APR   1997

RENOVATING WOMAN

A
GUIDE
TO HOME REPAIR,
MAINTENANCE
AND
REAL MEN

RENOVATING WOMAN

ALLEGRA BENNETT

POCKET BOOKS

New York   London   Toronto   Sydney   Tokyo   Singapore

Watercolors and line drawings by Vicki Maloney. Illustrations on pages 40, 43, 49, 51, 61, 89, 96, 115, 121, 144 and 166 by Tamika Green.

POCKET BOOKS, a division of Simon & Schuster Inc.
1230 Avenue of the Americas, New York, NY 10020

Library of Congress Cataloging-in-Publication Data
Bennett, Allegra.
   Renovating woman : a woman's guide to home repair, maintenance,
and real men / by Allegra Bennett.
     p. cm.
   ISBN 0-671-52771-1
   1. Dwellings—Maintenance and repair—Amateur's manuals.
2. Dwellings—Maintenance and repair—Anecdotes. I. Title.
TH4817.3.B46 1997
643'.7'082—dc20   96-42414
                                           CIP

First Pocket Books hardcover printing April 1997

10 9 8 7 6 5 4 3 2 1

POCKET and colophon are registered trademarks of
Simon & Schuster Inc.

Text design by Stanley S. Drate/Folio Graphics Co. Inc.

Printed in the U.S.A.

"Hard times will either make you or break you." My mother was fond of quotations and no doubt would have repeated that bromide to me often had she lived until I was old enough to have provoked it from her. This book was born out of hard times. Dorothy Delcina Nora Williams Brown was an amusing woman who would have been pleased to learn that her daughter did not break. She would have been thrilled to know her grand-daughter—my girl Alycia Dineen Bennett Taylor—whose pep chats and hilarious tales about her daughter, my grand, kept me going when I didn't think I could go anymore. My son, cool hand Jamal, listened quietly (I like to think intently, but that's a mother's fantasy) as his mother unburdened her fears in a daunting stream of consciousness. He soothed me every time with his confident grin and "You'll be a'ite," a phrase from the young person's lexicon of fractured English that under any other circumstance would make a mother throw a dictionary.

. . . Where Credit Is Due

As self-sufficient as I like to think I am, I nevertheless could not have produced this volume without the tireless generosity of many people. I sincerely hope I have given credit where it is due. But if I have been remiss, please be kind. The oversight is not due to malice or carelessness but rather Adult Onset Memory Lapse. I'm working on it.

Handy Coulbourn's career specialty is that of a master carpenter, but he is far more than that. He is an accidental professor who escorts a simple question on a marvelous tangent that produces wonderfully useful stuff. He continues to selflessly teach me what technical knowledge I need in the world of home improvement while introducing me to great words like "perspicacious."

Claude L. Sessoms Sr. is the original braveheart. As his unofficial apprentice, I learned firsthand how to put up a ceiling, put on a new roof, ask questions, never accept the first answer, recognize there is no time like the present, and be braver than I ever thought I could be.

When laughter was the only antidote to save me from manuscript malaise, Brenda Box Johnson and Debra Moore had me in much needed stitches. Both my friend Lydia Nayo's application for tenure as a law school professor and the manuscript for this book were due the same day. Playing out our coast-to-coast anxiety dramas was great, cheap therapy for us both.

. . . WHERE CREDIT IS DUE

Research maven Carolyn Hardnett can find anything, a fact she proved repeatedly. Esperance Sutton's mantra "Why not?" led me on terrific home improvement expeditions. News junkies Sue Kopen Katcef and Mark Miller of WBAL Radio gave Renovating Woman her first radio voice. Newsman Dan Rodricks gave her a face. Special thanks to Tod Lindberg whose low-maintenance management style freed my creativity.

Contents

CONTENTS

Introduction

While married, I was blissfully ignorant about the mysteries of home repair and maintenance. As far as I was concerned, the labyrinth of pipes and wires in the basement was a guy thing. So I happily left them to The Guy.

His job and my job were distinct. When the garbage disposal backed up, for instance, his job was to go into the basement and yell orders. My job was to follow his minimalist directions to position the plunger over the drain and shout back "Okay" after I'd filled the sink with water. A few minutes later he'd yell back, "Let it go." That was my cue to release the plunger. I did so gladly and happily resumed my traditional female role of taking care of the details of life for that day.

I can't tell you how The Guy spent the half hour he was down below. I had absolutely no curiosity about it so I never checked. All I know is when he reemerged the disposal worked—until the next time. He was the basement quarterback and I had no intention of running interference. However, there came a time when The Guy and this gal divorced and the chickens, as it were, came home to roost.

One morning in the early days of our divorcehood I shoved some shrimp heads down the disposal, forgetting that the appliance was wholly unreliable. It predictably acted up, causing an overflow in the drain that cascaded to the basement floor, taking a dozen ceiling tiles with it. I telephoned The Ex immediately, yielding to an instinct that had formed over the twenty-three years we have been husband and wife. His advice made my eyes cross. He said I would have to snake the main drain, aerate, establish a balanced mix of oxygen, and maybe he said throw horseshoes. I didn't know what he was talking about. Where was the main drain anyway? Whatever he was suggesting I wasn't going to do it.

After some preliminary whining I telephoned a few plumbers in the yellow pages. A few of their estimates provided the reality check I needed to startle me to my senses: $75 to ring the doorbell and $45 per quarter hour if they actually had to fix something. With no room for emergencies built into my finances it meant I would have to do the job myself. Armed with a new resolve, I slopped through the gray mess in the basement and removed the damaged panels from the drop ceiling just beneath the kitchen. Deductive reasoning led me to a white plastic pipe leading from the disposal and terminating at what turned out to be the main drain. Coming out of the drain was a black hose that led from the dishwasher, which also had a history of backflow. Our solution to that problem was to wash dishes the old-fashioned way.

I began tugging on the black hose so that I could pull it out and snake the drain, not really having a clue how effective the snake and I were going to be. A few seconds of hard tugging and pulling disclosed what no one in their right mind needs a $180 and hour plumber to figure out: The hose coming from the dishwasher was too long! It was blocking the throat of the drain, preventing all but a trickle from getting through. I didn't have to snake a thing. The solution was simple, I whacked about four inches off the hose, reinserted it into the drainpipe, and stabilized its positioning with a clamp. I dashed upstairs to the kitchen and ran a test. I turned on the water and with fingers crossed flipped the switch on the disposal and began shoving the remaining shrimp heads down the hopper. I detected no splashing sounds below. For the first time in two years, the thing worked. No obstruction. No backflow. Now emboldened I got clean dishes out of the cupboard and loaded up the dishwasher. No backup! Yahooey! Dare I run them together? I did. Freeflow! I was beside myself with joy. Hell, I was the maven of the universe. I'd finally achieved appliance peace in my home.

The Ex was not at home when I called him with my terrific progress report, so I left a detailed message on his answering machine and rewarded myself with a shopping spree for tools. When I returned a few hours later there was a message on my machine from The Ex. His voice rang with genuine wonder: "Oh," he exclaimed, "so that's what that black hose was!"

It was a crystal moment that changed me forever. I had spent all of my married years taking for granted that the male understanding of things mechanical was as naturally intuitive as a mother's instinct. But all along, the male's understanding was not as much intuition as bluff. That discovery was *the* liberating moment of my life. The Ex had made allies of his patience, my acquiescence, and my lack of curiosity. He also knew that if you waited long enough even the mighty Mississippi will drain. That was an epiphany of pivotal proportions. It armed me with a confidence that only could have evolved from successfully confronting the unknown head-on even while my knees were knocking. From that day forward I was a home repair victim no longer.

So, The Guy and the crippling crutch he provided were gone. But left behind like an albatross around my neck was the house and its myriad needs. And according to the last census I was not alone. There were nearly thirty-nine million women who because of divorce, widowhood, choice, or hammertoes were living without a male presence in the home. Several million of these women own their homes and their number is steadily increasing.

This is a relevant little factoid considering that women serve as typical marks for the unscrupulous fix-it man, whether or not there is a male presence. It gets worse when we are home alone. A woman's natural tendency toward cooperation rather than confrontation and her instinct to nurture feeds the schemes of the home repair predators. Ultimately, she helps conspire against her own best interest.

Unquestionably, living alone has intimidating moments, particularly when a house function breaks down. Lack of familiarity fuels fears that are crippling. The older the house, the more frequent the breakdowns, the greater the intimidation.

However, it does not have to be that way. Self-confidence is a powerful elixir. Since my emotional renovation, my basement ceased to daunt me the way it once did. I became curious about and familiar with its workings. I even built a workshop down there. I own an assortment of power tools and I know how to use them, including my delightful chain saw. I'm something to see with that in my hands!

However, overcoming one's fears takes a bit of strategy. You have to cast the dread in familiar terms. Houses are much like human relationships. Some are easygoing, like some men. And some houses are like petulant lovers who stockpile their resentments, eventually releasing them in one explosive tirade. Houses are alive. They are perpetually shifting and settling and consequently require constant maintenance to prevent irreversible breakdowns like the furnace that one day suddenly gasped and quit on me.

The house was cold and I didn't know where to begin. It was not until $4,000 and a new furnace later that I learned that my steam radiator heating system meant I should have been periodically flushing the boiler to clear it of the rust that collects and often clogs the furnace's water intake line. A little maintenance would have prevented that expensive lesson. But I didn't know. And it never occurred to me to ask maintenance questions while everything was running just fine.

Invariably, when we do ask the right questions they are almost always in the heat of an emergency. And even in an age of high feminine consciousness, women still tend to seek out male counsel—even total strangers—when it comes to the mechanically driven. And then, we accept these representations without question.

It's a conditioning that I figure began centuries ago when gladiators and knights were forming muscles and the male mystique. Despite the historical marketing hype, the chariot races and jousting tournaments of yore were nothing more than mindless weekend sports. Those guys may have looked and performed like toned behemoths, but flabby logic is flabby logic.

Renovating Woman will help women rely on themselves first to handle those chores we have conceded to others to our own detriment. Restoring a wall or fixing a faucet, for example, has mending properties that go beyond the obvious. Those moments are opportunities for therapeutic time-outs from that which is not so easily patched over—a demanding family, a challenging career, a rocky romance, financial hurdles, and a score of other invasions that make life, life. Many a woman might even discover that the solitary task of repairing a crack in the Sheetrock or stilling a drip in a faucet provides quiet time for healing the cracks and stilling the drips that vex her pysche.

What's more, the single woman who earnestly undertakes the care and feeding of her home will make a fun discovery. Her new acquisition of the language of home repair will put her in touch with the kind of male pulchritude that previously existed only in the fantasy factory of her mind. She will discover the world of the "real man."

Renovating Woman is for the Everywoman faced with maintenance and basic repair jobs at home whether she lives alone or with someone who doesn't know an awl from an owl. It celebrates the transition, inventiveness, and evolution of the woman, a creature who proves to be enormously adaptable once she is able to trade knowledge for fear.

Before You Even Begin . . .

Reading the Rule

I used to suffer from fraction phobia. Way back in elementary school I was never really compelled to learn to recognize more than the 1/4-, 1/2-, and 3/4-inch measurement of a whole number on a ruler, and my teachers didn't seem to care whether we girls learned to measure with any more accuracy than that. When we came to a measurement that fell on one of those tiny foreign lines, we simply rounded off to the nearest quarter measure and said "and some." So that 1 and 5/16ths would be "1 and 1/4 and some."

Well, rounding off may be an acceptable practice for passing elementary school math or computing tax returns, but it can amount to a serious shortcoming if you are relying on that measurement for the proper fit of a wall-to-wall shelf. I abandoned many a project to rule ruin because of my fraction phobia. Way into adulthood when I was forced into a situation of exactitude by a co-worker I reported a measurement of 4 and 5/8ths inches, for example, as "4 inches and two tick marks past one-half." It was a little less ethereal than "and some" but ridiculous nonetheless. My measuring style always drew a laugh, but I felt foolish later knowing that I did approximations because I didn't know how to read the tick marks. It was tantamount to signing my name with an X.

One day when I got tired of a failing that I had the power to do some-

Tale of the Tape

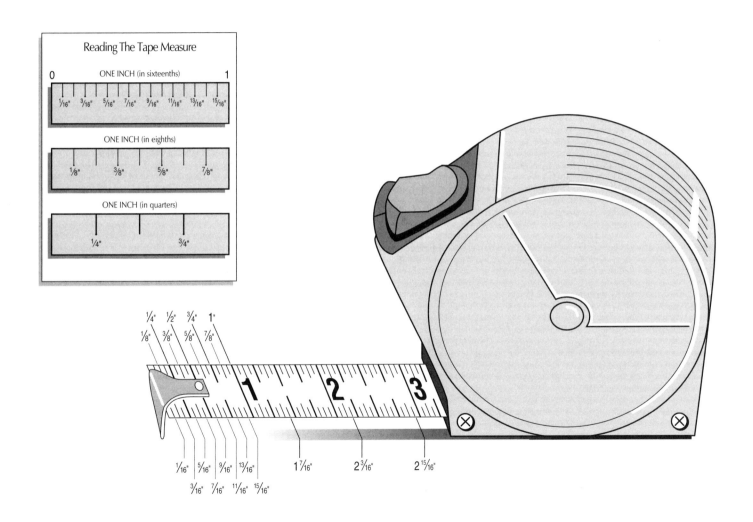

thing about, I forced myself past my math anxiety and learned the names of the tiny lines on the ruler. Just in case you had the same teachers I had, here's how it works:

On the standard 25-foot handygal one-inch metal pullout tape measure there are sixteen lines between each inch. The first short mark, or gradient, after the solid-line inch mark is 1/16th. Following the rules of basic math for fractions, reduce the reading to the least common denominator (LCD).

$^1/_{16}$th			$^9/_{16}$ths	
$^2/_{16}$ths $=$ $^1/_8$th	(LCD)		$^{10}/_{16}$ths $=$ $^5/_8$ths	(LCD)
$^3/_{16}$ths			$^{11}/_{16}$ths	
$^4/_{16}$ths $=$ $^1/_4$	(LCD)		$^{12}/_{16}$ths $=$ $^3/_4$ths	(LCD)
$^5/_{16}$ths			$^{13}/_{16}$ths	
$^6/_{16}$ths $=$ $^3/_8$ths	(LCD)		$^{14}/_{16}$ths $=$ $^7/_8$ths	(LCD)
$^7/_{16}$ths			$^{15}/_{16}$ths	
$^8/_{16}$ths $=$ $^1/_2$	(LCD)		$^{16}/_{16}$ths $=$ 1 inch	(LCD)

RENOVATING WOMAN

1

THE NAME IS HALF THE GAME

Talk the Talk

When it comes to calling the parts of a house by their proper names the vocabulary is sparingly utilitarian for most of us. You have your doors, your windows, your walls, and your floors. For the other stuff between the roof and the cellar floor "whatchamacallit" and "thingamabob" are wondrously pragmatic. We figure if you're not in the building trades, what more do you need to know? Of course, the answer is "plenty."

Once upon a time I had no emotional commitment whatever to knowing, for example, that a roof comprises several parts bearing distinct names and duties. Flashing, for instance, is a thin piece of sheet metal typically found around the chimney and valleys of the roof. Its job is to prevent water from seeping into the seams, valleys, and hip connections on the roof. To me, so what? It was simply a roof part worthy of no singular distinction or mention. But dealing with contractors is much like attending a Washington cocktail party. You want to drop names. It gives you the appearance of authority and interest, which are two major elements in the negotiations between women and male contractors.

If you were having a conversation with a roofing contractor ("roofer" in contractor lingo) about a leaky chimney or the wall to which it is attached, for example, you'd want to mention flashing by its name. It can be a costly tactical error not to, as I discovered when I needed roof work involving the area around the chimney. My chats with the contractors I interviewed to do the job were precious.

"What's the problem, ma'am?" they'd ask for starters. (I hate it when they "ma'am" me.) "I need the roof fixed," I'd say plaintively. "That part over there, see, near the chimney, by the grayish thing with the sunken look and the metal thingamabob. See, stand over here. Okay, see where the robin just flew over? See where it dropped the twig? No, on the first bounce. Yeah, right there."

Mr. Roofer took a deep drag on his cigarette and slowly blew it out, making a soft whistling sound as he stared up past the clouds. He had the smug, faraway look of someone who knew he had won the lottery and was just biding his time on a make-work job until he cashed in his winning ticket. In effect he *had* just won the lottery and my pocketbook was the take.

It's funny how things work out. The contractor's distant gaze happened to remind me of a trip I had taken to Japan some years earlier. In preparation for the trip I studied a few opening phrases and as a backup took along a pocketbook-sized Berlitz dictionary for travelers—a habit I employed in my visits to many other countries. The Japanese I met were impressed that I at least tried to communicate in their language. My efforts were rewarded with personal invitations during my short stay that allowed me insights into the culture that were not available to us *gaijings* (foreigners) on the usual sterile tourist trail. Since vocabulary is a universal door opener in any language, I decided to apply my foreign travel approach to the exotic world of home repair contractors.

A sympathetic whistle-blower once confided to me that labor is the largest, most fluid portion of a contractor's bill. They can fiddle with the cost of material to some degree by charging you for leftover material that the customer from the last job already paid for. But they really hit pay dirt with labor. They put an arbitrary price on their sweat, then add as much as a 50 percent premium for your ignorance.

By referring to house parts by their proper names, a homeowner brings balance to the table and transforms a price dictum into a dynamic negotiation between an employer and a potential employee, you being the employer, a point which tends to escape us in the heat of negotiation. The price is always negotiable. The first figures are merely the opening bid.

Calling objects by their names is the best defense short of knowing how to do the job yourself. When you use the proper nomenclature, contractors will at least wonder if you know as much as your vocabulary suggests. With thingamabob and whatchamacallit they know for sure.

Arm Yourself

Finding out the names of objects is as simple as going around to home project centers, reading the labels on the packages, and talking to clerks about specific jobs. Browse through their collection of home repair and project books or buy a video. Check books out at the library. Many secondhand bookstores have whole sections of home how-to books at affordable prices. Pay attention to the language. Use your newfound vocabulary with unabashed regularity. Strike up conversations with friends about home repair. You'll be surprised at what they know, although you should take for granted nothing that they say. Question everything. Check it out through an independent source. After all, you will be new at this, and there are folks who thrill at the sound of their own voices even though they are singing off key.

Anyone who lives indoors should have on the shelf at home a reference book on appliances and the maintenance and repair of basic utilities in their dwelling. A book like *Renovating Woman* is essential for starters.

You'll want to thumb through these books and note the basic language of the household plumbing and electricity, for example. Emergencies happen. However, when they do, you don't want to panic and dial up the first handyman in the yellow pages. Resist succumbing to the initial terror of a flooded basement or leaky roof. Get out the book. Look up the possible causes and remedies and, most of all, note and quickly rehearse the language before hiring help, if hiring help is even necessary, and most times it won't be. Familiarity often is the critical difference between what you spend and what you get to keep in your purse.

Dress Rehearsal

One other way to learn contractor talk that I highly recommend is to rehearse the job yourself.

I was going to hire someone to replace my porch roof and decided to get an idea of the cost of material and the work involved before I began soliciting bids. I approximated the size of the roof and went to the home project center with a head full of questions.

The experts there told me I would need at least twelve bundles of shingles (see, they call them bundles, not packs), a roll of 15-weight roofing paper, ten pounds of roofing nails, and three tubes of roofing cement. The total cost of the materials was $95. The estimates I received to do the job ranged from $1,800 to $3,500. Knowing what I learned about the price of materials, I couldn't bring myself to shell out possibly $3,405 more than necessary.

I had never done a roof before. But it's amazing how brave you become when (1) you're broke and (2) someone tells you "if another human being can do it so can you," as did my friend who had done a roof or two. Fortunately he is the kind of guy who thinks women should reduce their exposure to victimhood. He volunteered to show me how to do the job. I went for it.

As the new kid on the job I was assigned the grunt work, fetching tools and carrying the bundles of tiles up to the roof. Because I was afraid of climbing the twenty-foot stilt of a ladder, I approached the porch roof from a second-floor bedroom window and handed the tiles out to my teacher on the roof. Well, that couldn't last. For one, I could tell that the initial amusement the teacher felt about my cowardice was wearing thin and I could not learn the task simply by handing him stuff out the window. I had to come out and perform. For another, I was wearing myself out picking up a stack of tiles, hauling them up the front steps into the house, across the entry hall, up another flight of steps, through another hallway, and all the way across the room to the window. On the way down, the kitchen proved a distraction, since every time I came near it I stopped by the refrigerator or cabinet for a quick snack to pop in my mouth. What's more, I was beginning to track roofing debris on the stairway carpeting, which would have been a bear to clean up. I finally dug deep and found the courage to go up the ladder and step out on the roof. It wasn't long before I didn't even think about the fact that I was walking on a twenty-five-degree angle, and after about fifteen round-trips, climbing the shaky twenty-foot ladder seemed as natural as walking up a stairway.

Inspect the Work

Now, even if you decide not to do the roof work yourself, you must oversee the task and get involved in the process. You still should inspect the job and any other jobs you contract out—before and after the work is completed. Before-and-after photos are great tools. Either photograph the area before and after yourself or have the contractor you decide to hire photograph the problem area before starting the job and again upon completion. You provide the camera and film, of course. Instant shots are ideal.

The nerve it took for me to do my porch roof myself didn't grow overnight. That evolution had begun about a year earlier. At that time, the upper roof was a problem. It required replacing several slate tiles and sealing gaps along the roof joints or hips with roofing cement. The job also called for closing up the equal-opportunity condo the pigeons and squirrels had set up in the eaves. That meant replacing the rotting facia boards along one side of the house and cleaning the debris out of the gutters and reseating them. I hired someone to do the job.

The workmen made it a one-day affair. They arrived before seven that morning and by four o'clock, supposedly finished, they started packing up. They took down the intricate scaffolding and packed it away on the truck. Then the foreman came to the door with his clipboard, ticked off an allegedly completed list of repairs, pronounced the roof good for another ten years, and rocked back on his heels waiting for payment.

Back then, when it came to work on the roof, I preferred the trust-in-my-fellow-man approach. After all, that level of roof was more than forty feet off the ground. I reached for the clipboard to look over the list and sign my approval. But just as I was about to sign off I heard a familiar voice say, "I'd like to inspect the job." The voice was mine.

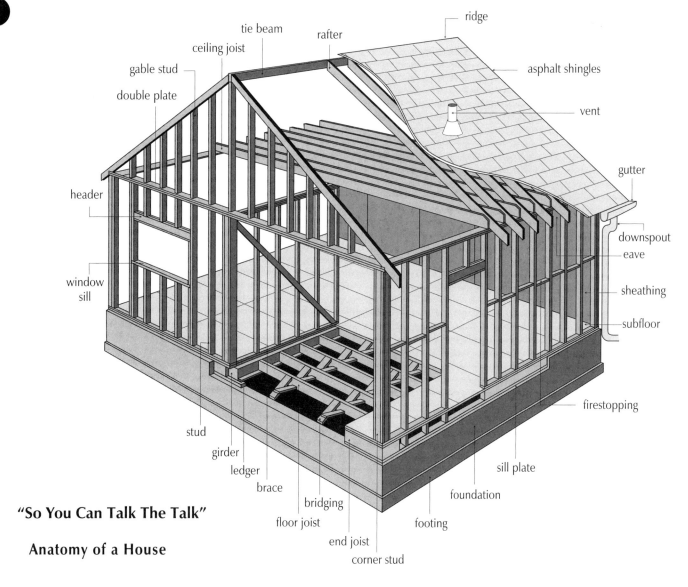

ridge

tie beam

rafter

ceiling joist

gable stud

asphalt shingles

double plate

vent

header

gutter

window sill

downspout

eave

sheathing

subfloor

firestopping

stud

girder

ledger

brace

bridging

floor joist

sill plate

foundation

end joist

footing

corner stud

"So You Can Talk The Talk"

Anatomy of a House

I felt both frightened and exhilarated by my bold demand. My mind raced with the possibilities. This was no movie. If I went up there and fell off the ladder, it would not be a stunt double but dummy me who hits the concrete. I hoped that somehow, something or someone would prevent me from going through with it.

"You want to go up there?" the foreman asked with a decided mocking edge to his voice. The mocking did it. I took the bait.

"Yes," I said firmly.

"But we already took the rig down," he said.

That was my out, but my prideful ego kept my mouth moving. "Well, set up one of the forty-footers," I said mimicking what I had overheard him command the guys earlier.

Still smirking, the foreman yanked one of the forty-foot ladders off the truck rack. His helpers set it up against the house. I went back inside, asked myself if I was crazy, gripped my stomach and grabbed my gloves. I thought about sassy Mae West. She would be up that ladder, wide-brimmed picture hat, lace gloves, bustle, and all. Of course, she'd have something cleverly withering to say along the way like: "Stand back, boys. This job calls for talent." Back outside I put my gloves on and took to the ladder, petrified.

Mr. Smirk stepped aside and held the ladder as I began my ascent. I'd never been on the top end of a forty-foot ladder before, but I climbed this one, all along the way talking trash about how I just knew I was going to see they had done a fine job. The higher I went the lighter the air became. My head felt spacey, my stomach queasy, and the thought of my mortality and my grief-stricken children consumed my mind. I figured I was risking a lot for a bluff.

At the top, to steady myself, I gripped the roof ledge. I turned my head slowly left then right to ward off vertigo and panic. Enough was enough.

I figured I'd better get down before I fell down. I slowly backed down the ladder praying I wouldn't black out before I reached the ground.

By the time my foot touched the bottom rung of the ladder my head started to clear. I stepped down, still faking bravado but feeling like whipped cream inside and, worst of all, not knowing what the heck I saw up on the roof. My fear had blinded me.

Finally on the ground, I put one arm akimbo. With the other hand I pinched the corners of my eyes at the bridge of my nose and turned my head slowly back and forth still trying to recover my internal balance. Before I could utter a word Mr. Smirk sheepishly sputtered: "Oh, I saw you shaking your head up there. Did we miss something?"

"Oh yeah, boss," one of his helpers chimed in, mumbling a confession about how he thought he may have forgotten to get back to this side of the house. "Sorry, ma'am, we seem to have missed a few spots," the foreman said. "Why don't we take care of that while we have the ladder up?" There was absolutely no trace of the cockiness in his voice nor the arrogant demeanor that had forced me to make the climb.

It was a delicious moment. A moment of power. The power of the unexpected. The power of bluff. The power of results. It was as close as I would come to a testosterone surge. I had just won a decisive fight for turf.

I said nothing at first, deciding to soak the moment for its drama. I gave the foreman a hard stare through eyes that were still out of focus. "Yeah," I said with as much of a dramatic pause as I could muster without breaking into a smirk myself. "I noticed. Why don't you just take care of that little thing?" With deliberation, I removed my gloves, tucked them in the back pockets of my jeans, and headed back inside walking the walk, popping one knee as if I had a pebble in my shoe just like the neighborhood tough guy. Yes!

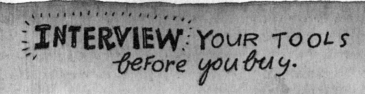

2

NO MORE BUTTER KNIVES

Everyone should have a loaded toolbox whether they are renting an apartment or own a house. Of course, few people really own houses. Banks own houses. People own the late charges and the maintenance problems. For the latter you need to have a toolbox ready and outfitted with the right stuff.

My first toolbox was a cigar box of junk. I didn't consult it much, so I wasn't aware that the flathead screwdriver that was in there had a rusted tip and the small pipe wrench that kept it company was good for no repair job worthy of the name.

Nothing will make you more keenly aware of your shortcomings faster than the need for something you should have but don't. Like the time I was doing a small project involving laminate that required a utility knife, a basic tool for every household.

I had built a vanity for the bathroom sink out of pressboard and planned to laminate the sides to eliminate that "this is a do-it-yourself-and-don't-I-look-like-it" project. A razor-sharp blade to score the laminate was necessary, but I had no such tool. What should have been utility turned to futility.

Since I was trying to get the job done before the walk-through of potential home buyers, I had to implement Plan B. I ended up slapping white glossy paint where laminate was supposed to go. The paint job didn't look as good as laminate, nor did it provide the waterproofing or durability of laminate. Take a bit of advice from the Boy Scouts' motto and "Be prepared."

Your toolbox and shelf should be a mix of tools that are both power driven and manual. Power tools are terrific inventions. They are fast and make work easier. Nonetheless, a toolbox is not a toolbox without the traditional hand tools. There will be times when the power tool is impractical while working in tight spaces or doing delicate work.

As you become familiar with tools, you will discover that it is not enough to ask someone to pass you the hammer, the pliers, the screwdriver, or the wrench.

There are as many as five different kinds of hammers, six types of pliers, ten types of screwdrivers, and forget about wrenches, they multiply like guppies. Of course, you don't need to have them all. There are about twenty tools and supplies you should have on hand; the others you can buy or rent as you need them. For starters one of the most critical tools every woman ought to have prominently displayed is **attitude.** You can't buy it. It comes with practice.

No woman should ever face a contractor without it. Society has conditioned women to defer to men in certain situations even when they are wrong. It's a benign behavior in social settings but decidedly crippling when the two genders are negotiating business. It is important to develop a gutsy posture that at least sounds like you are in charge even if you're not sure *yet*.

You may not be able to fill your toolbox with all you need at once. That can be a costly proposition. But there are some items you ought to have on hand at a minimum.

First, **the box.** You'll want one that's heavy-duty with a removable tray. Rubbermaid makes a great one with a recessed handle that doubles as a step stool. The color doesn't matter except as it comports with your personal taste. If lavender is your color, run with it. But don't settle for pretty over substance.

Which brings us to this point. A color complex is probably the big reason contractors don't take women seriously. Men stick with stark black, green, white, and browns. Women like to flirt with the rainbow, giving some people the mistaken impression they are little balls of fluff. I came to this conclusion during an outing at a hardware store. The storekeeper was trying out a Mother's Day marketing gimmick.

He put together a toolbox with basic tools and targeted them to women. It was a great idea. He chose boxes in what he told me he thought were feminine colors—pink, lavender, periwinkle. Apron colors. That was fine. However, he seemed to think that meant any old box would do as long as the color was loud.

He selected a lightweight plastic thing that couldn't hold a season's supply of eyeshadow. This Renovating Woman had to inform him of his folly. If a woman is going to reach for a loaded toolbox she's serious. Just like any man, she wants to be confident that she's going to come away with more than the handle in her hand.

The storekeeper apologized, saying he had his wife's makeup case in mind . . . as if makeup ain't serious. By the time I left he learned that women take their makeup seriously too. Every woman knows that when she wants to put on a face, she goes to the makeup case. When she wants to fix a leaky faucet, she goes to the toolbox. And it doesn't matter if either box is pink, lavender, or periwinkle. It is the box's substance that matters.

Mary Kay Asher wears a pink suit and drives a pink Cadillac, but backing her up is a pile of greenbacks that came from makeup. Substance had a lot to do with it.

A properly outfitted basic toolbox would contain at the very least:

Work gloves: For obvious reasons you should wear gloves and keep a couple pair on hand. They can be made of canvas or leather, but always have at least one pair made of rubber. You'll notice that for reasons only they understand men don't like to wear gloves. They prefer to slop their hands around in grime of undetermined origin and clean up later with a product that has a skull and crossbones on the label. However, hands should be protected no matter whose hands they are. The fingernail beds are vulnerable to injury. You will eventually learn how to patch a wall expertly and put up a ceiling yourself, but you don't want your hands to feel like that's what you've been doing all along.

Knee pads: To protect your knees and shins from looking like an alligator purse.

Goggles: To protect your eyes.

Dust mask: To protect your respiratory system.

Tape measure: The best kind is a retractable model at least twenty-five feet in length made of flexible steel with a lock button to hold the tape in place while it is extended.

Adhesives such as wood glue or bond are good reinforcement for items joined with screws or nails. A product called Liquid Nails, in particular, forms a tight bond between two pieces of wood, which then allows for easier, more efficient driving of screws. Sometimes on small jobs, adhesives alone are sufficient.

3-in-one-oil or WD40 is perfect for eliminating squeaks fast or loosening a stuck drawer.

String is the handiest, most versatile tool ever. It performs a host of tasks from bundling old newspapers to drawing perfect circles to sizing a wall.

Scissors for the usual snip-and-cut chore.

Utility knife is aptly named. Its supersharp blade can make quick work of cutting paper or plastic or scoring soft metals and wallboard. The blade is retractable and the knife is available in a plastic or heavy metal casing. The metal model is best. A storage compartment in the body safekeeps extra blades. Each blade has two sharp ends. When you've worked one end until it's dull, open the handle, carefully flip the blade so that the sharp end protrudes from the handle, and you're in business again.

Duct tape can be used to wrap a pipe or repair the kids' athletic shoes.

Sandpaper is used for a variety of smoothing tasks on wood and metals. It comes in coarse, medium, and light grains.

Nails and **screws** of varying lengths and types are great to have on hand. Screws are preferable when there's a choice because they provide a tighter hold and the material is less likely to shift and twist out of place over time.

A **putty knife** comes in narrow and wide styles and is used to apply paste or perform light scraping tasks on peeling surfaces. You should have a wide and a narrow version.

An **awl,** pronounced "all," is a small, sharp, pointed tool whose sole purpose is to start the holes for driving in nails or screws. Just puncture the target spot on the wood where the nail or screw is to go and then drive in the screw. You can ruin a good piece of wood or spoil a job if you try to drive a nail or screw into a spot that has not been prepared with an awl.

A **claw hammer** weighing no more than sixteen ounces. A heavier one might seem logical for some jobs but will wear your arm out before you can get the job done.

Pliers (3): A **needle-nose** (also called long-nose) model with a wire cutter feature; a **blunt-nose** model and a **slip-joint** ten-inch model.

Screwdrivers: A variety package containing a Phillips head tip and a flathead tip (also called slot tip).

Wrench: A ten-inch adjustable one.

Level: One about twelve inches in length is large enough for starters. Use it to assure that the shelf goes up straight. It's more reliable than eyeballing a job. Typically, your eyes see a level shelf but the sliding books tell a different story. Levels come in many types and sizes, from three inches to four feet long and often are referred to as carpenter's levels.

A **heavy-duty stapler** is great for a variety of tacking tasks. Stereo speaker wire can be discreetly stapled along baseboards and chairs can get a new face with fresh fabric tacked on the seat frame. And, if you're truly trifling, you can staple rather than paste wallpaper, though I wouldn't advise it. I've seen this. I've done it myself. It's not pretty. I reverted to paste. But have a bad day with the kids, the job, the husband, or the significant other and a woman is liable to turn a bulldozer on the house. So staple the wallpaper if you like.

Cordless or electric drill: $3/8$ths reversible model with drill bits and adapters.

Just So You'll Know

HAMMERS come in several styles and weights. Measured in ounces, they can be as light as seven ounces and as heavy as thirty-two. The best hammer heads are made of drop-forged steel. Drop-forged is a hardening process in steel manufacturing that produces steel with a particularly hard surface and durability. You want that in something you'll be repeatedly banging against hard objects.

The *curved claw* is the most common hammer. It's good for working with wood and driving and pulling nails and other fasteners. It is a good starter hammer and may be the only one you will ever need in the toolbox. But having more than one on hand for varying uses is wise.

Utility knife

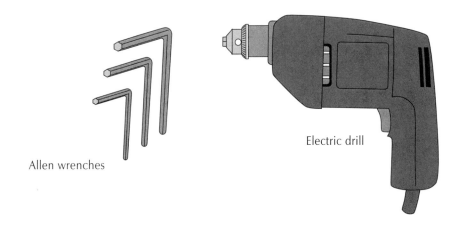

Allen wrenches

Electric drill

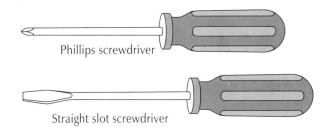

Phillips screwdriver

Straight slot screwdriver

Level

**RENOVATING
WOMAN**

Diagonal-cutting pliers

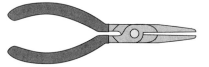

Needle-nose pliers

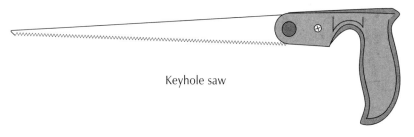

Keyhole saw

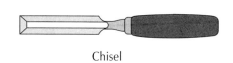

Chisel

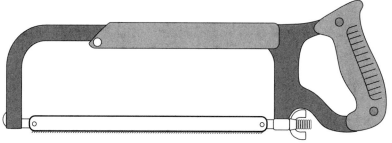

Hacksaw

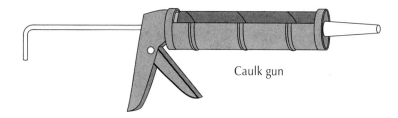

Caulk gun

NO MORE BUTTER KNIVES

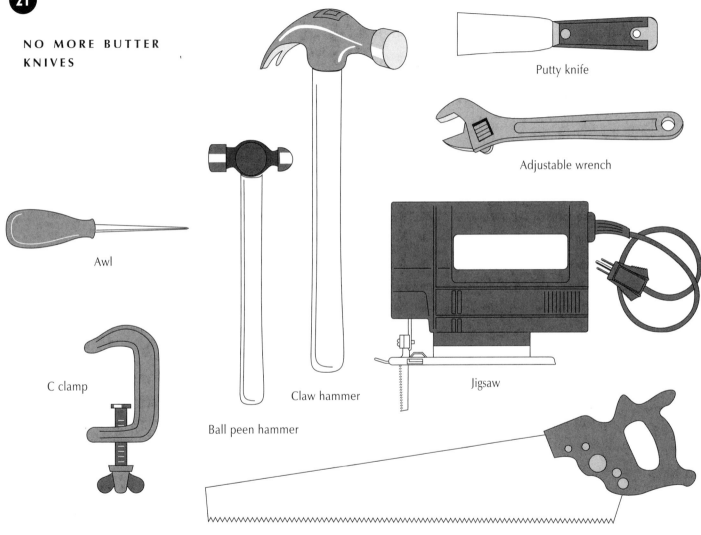

Putty knife

Adjustable wrench

Awl

Jigsaw

C clamp

Claw hammer

Ball peen hammer

Crosscut saw

The *straight claw* is designed for ripping and prying, as in opening heavy wooden or metal boxes and crates. Consequently, it is a heavy hammer weighing up to thirty-two ounces.

The *ball peen* has a rounded head and is a good choice when working on metal.

The *tack hammer* with its narrow handle and heavy, slender metal head is a specialty tool perfect for driving tacks in upholstering jobs. Its small, weighty design allows for striking tacks directly on the head and into place on a chair seat, for example, without harming the wood frame.

Mallets can be made of rubber, plastic, or wood. They are great for banging or shaping metal without marring the metal's surface. They're also excellent for cracking crab and lobster claws without splintering and scattering the shells on the folks nearby.

SCREWDRIVERS come in many different types and scores of sizes. For every type there is another to which people in the trades can introduce you. It is not enough to have one screwdriver at home.

Have an array of styles and sizes. This is because you have to match the screwdriver to screw size so that the tip properly fits the slots in the screw heads. Screws driven with an undersized screwdriver can damage the heads, which are comparatively soft metal. You may be able to fit an oversized screwdriver into a slot head but you may damage the work. Hardware stores sell screwdriver sets with multiple-size tips.

To drive a number of screws rapidly by hand, a *spiral ratchet screwdriver* is wonderful. Pushing down on the handle spins the blade of this model, relieving your wrist of the hard work of driving the screws. It's the next best screwdriver short of a power-driven one.

A *flat or slotted head* screwdriver has a standard blade with a straight, flat tip for general use.

A *Phillips or cross head* has an *X* design on its tip and is used to drive screws with the same design.

A *jeweler's* screwdriver has a very soft tip. It is used for very fine work, typically on jewelry and electronic equipment affixed with very tiny screws.

WRENCHES get a grip on nuts, bolts, spark plugs. There are more than a dozen styles. Here are four of many popular ones.

An *adjustable end wrench* is a versatile wrench can be opened to fit many sizes of nuts, bolts, or pipes.

The *pipe wrench* is a heavy tool used to loosen large pipe connections.

Socket wrenches are short, column-shaped tubes that attach to a *ratchet* handle and fit over various-sized nuts. The socket wrench is great for working in awkward corners.

The *Allen wrench* is a thin L-shaped tool with a hexagonal tip designed to fit into screws with recessed hexagonal heads.

PLIERS are designed for gripping and pinching and are available in six styles. However, there are only three you are likely to ever need.

Needle nose or *long nose* for working within a narrow space.

Channel locks pivot into a number of positions with a jaw opening up to two inches. It will grip almost any shape.

Slip joint is the familiar one used for little jobs. Its mouth adjusts to varying widths.

WASHERS are thin rings of rubber, plastic, paper, or metal used generally in nut-and-bolt assemblies. The washer ring is used as a buffer between the assembled parts to relieve friction, ensure tightness, and prevent leakage. The washer would be the equivalent of the tiny rubber pieces women slip onto the poles of cheap pierced earrings to keep the metal of costume jewelry from turning the earlobe green.

A **CARPENTER'S LEVEL** that is a foot or two in length will do for home work. The level is made of a wood, aluminum, or magnesium frame that is about four inches high. Vials built into the frame contain a liquid with a bubble. The lengthwise vials are for checking horizontal surfaces. The level is held up against a wall or placed on a shelf and maneuvered until the bubble sits squarely between the two markings on the vial. That positioning signals that the area is level with the horizon. Vials that run crosswise are called plumb and are used for checking the levelness of vertical positions.

A **WIRE BRUSH** comes in handy for scraping away flaking or peeling paint, or rust.

Safety Gear—Just in Case You Think You Don't Need Any

While I was waiting in line at Motor Vehicles one morning I overheard the clerk instructing an elderly man standing at the counter to look into the vision tester and read the top line of the eye chart. But the man stared with his mouth hung open as though he was out in left field awaiting the arrival of a ten-mile-an-hour fly ball.

The clerk patiently strung out her usually brisk instructions to give the man time to catch on. "Look into the lens . . . and read . . . the first line . . . of the eye chart for me please," she said.

"Can't see no line," the man answered.

"Do you have both of your eyes open?" the clerk asked.

"He's only got one," the woman with him chimed in. "Other one's glass." Me and three strangers on the line doubled over trying to smother our laughter in our coats. The man was renewing his driver's license, after all.

That episode was a stitch. But, of course, losing an eye is no joke. There are all kinds of ways to do it. And most happen in the safety of the home in preventable accidents. You're in a hurry and figure it'll take just a minute to fire up the power saw and rip two inches off a board (that's construction talk for cutting the board). But in a split second the saw can flick sharp splinters into your eyes.

Invest in eyeguards. Even if you wear glasses, wear the guards over them. Eyeglasses shield most of the eye straight on but, true to form, trouble finds the first opening. Eyeguards provide protection for the sides as well. Exercise a little caution and you won't have to get fitted for a glass eye.

On the Side

A six-foot **ladder** is great for the average home with ten-foot-high ceilings. Get one with a fold-down stage near the top step on which to rest a paint can or bucket. The stage should feature a few predrilled holes through which a hammer or screwdriver can be suspended. That will decrease the number of trips up and down the ladder for the forgotten whatever. What with cathedral ceilings a popular choice in new home construction, an **EXTENDABLE** twenty-foot ladder would be good to have in the garage or basement. A **STEP STOOL** is great for quickie trips up. A pair of **COLLAPS-IBLE SAWHORSES** made of metal or wood are great as racks for balancing long planks of wood during cutting jobs. They fold flat for easy storage.

On the Shelf

A **UTILITY BELT:** There's something sensual and quixotic about a utility belt. Men look so virile when they are all hitched up in one of those multi-pocketed leather models with a hammer on each hip, screwdrivers, tape measures, and all sorts of other tool stuff suspended from everywhere.

Some women report that strapping a utility belt around their waists gives them a stimulating flush in their cheeks not unlike slipping on naughty apparel.

From a nonprurient, practical standpoint, however, the utility belt is the equivalent of wearing a lightweight toolbox around your waist. The belt helps you to organize yourself for the task at hand, limiting the number of trips for the forgotten or misplaced tool. I prefer the **CARPENTER'S APRON,** which is a canvas version of the leather model. Leather tends to get hot and heat up your skin, thereby making the task uncomfortable.

HANDSAWS: As with anything in life there's cheap and there's high quality. Start off with high quality and you'll never get stuck with a tool that can't do the job. That rule is particularly important to note with handsaws. A saw's performance depends a lot on its quality. A dull saw is very discouraging. A high-quality saw is precision ground to tiny points that allow nice sharp cuts across the wood fibers.

A cheap saw can make your arm fatigue very quickly. The number of teeth or points per inch typically range from seven to twelve. A saw with a low point number leaves a rough cut. The higher the number the more teeth per inch and the smoother the finished cut.

CROSSCUT saws are used for cutting wood across the grain. To begin a cut, start at the butt portion of the blade near the handle, using several pulling strokes to cut a groove. That done, don't cut right on the line. Position the saw to the throwaway or waste side of the line, as this minimizes cutting too short, and take full, broad strokes for fast, even cutting.

HACKSAWS typically are used to cut metal. The blades are thin and fit a rigid frame that is eight to twelve inches long. The removable blade is held in place with a wing nut.

A **HOLE SAW** has a set of circular blades to cut holes of varying dimensions up to about two and a half inches in circumference.

A **CAULK GUN** is used to apply puttylike material around the edge of a bathtub, shower, or windows to seal out moisture.

A **PLUNGER** has a long wood handle attached to a rubber disk used to unstop drains and toilets with a suction pressure.

A **VICE GRIP** is like an aggressive bill collector. It squeezes objects together to force a bonding.

A **C-CLAMP** is similar to the vise grip but offers a wider opening. It holds objects in place while you are sawing or joining.

Power Tools

Forget diamonds. Power tools truly are a gal's best friend around the house. These guys work fast and make a job way easier to do. If you've never handled a power tool before and would like to own one one day, here's what you do. Find someone who already owns the tool you're interested in and have them show you how to use it. Just holding a five-pound vibrating saw in your hands for the first time can be unsettling. Some vibration is expected. However, if it's lofting you out of your shoes, that may be a little too much quiver. You will want to get accustomed to the shake, rattle, and roll before you tackle a job.

You might think you don't know anyone with power tools but you'd be surprised who has what in their closets when you start asking. Nonetheless, you can always hit the hardware or home repair departments and engage one of the experts to demonstrate the tool and let you handle it. Don't wait until you need the tool to find out how it feels because you don't want to be in a hurry when you buy it. Take your time and get acquainted with the prospective purchase just the way you would (or should) that new man you want in your life.

CIRCULAR SAWS are terrific for fast cutting—or ripping, as they say in the trade—boards. The most practical model is a seven and a quarter inch with an automatic blade guard, an adjustable baseplate, and a saw blade depth adjustment. The saws usually are sold with a combination blade that can cut with the wood grain (lengthwise) or across the grain. But it's best to buy blades that are designed for specific cuts. The blades are sold for cutting plywood, doing crosscuts, or ripping.

The **CHAIN SAW** was my very first real power tool. It remains my favorite. If you have trees you'll want one of these impressive bad boys. You won't be able to slice through an aging redwood with ones sold for home use, but they can cut through a ten-inch tree limb like the ones typically found in the backyard in a pair of seconds. They use electric or gas power, and the chain is mounted on a twelve- to sixteen-inch bar. Most models have a safety feature that automatically turns the saw off it there is a jam. Periodically the chain slips off the bar, but it is easy to reseat after disengaging the power source. I took my delightful chain saw to a couple of dying fruit trees in my yard one year and had a ball.

The **POWER DRILL** comes in cordless or electric. The cordless offers great flexibility for use where no electricity is available. Some cordless models come with a battery pack and can be charged overnight. Both models are good to have on hand. They come in three sizes—$1/4$ inch, $3/8$ inch, and $1/2$ inch.

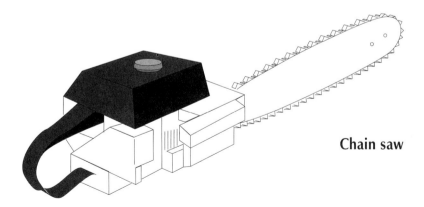

Chain saw

The drills use interchangeable tips known as bits that are used to drill or start pilot holes as well. The slotted (flathead) and Phillips head screwdriver tips also fit into the head when the job calls for a power screwdriver. The inch reference refers to the maximum-size drill bits the tool uses. The $^3/_8$-inch size is the most versatile for at-home jobs.

Aa Bb Cc Dd Ee Ff Gg Hh Ii Jj
I must turn off the power at the main switch
I must turn off the power at the
I must turn off the power at
I must turn off the power
I must

3

POWER TO THE PEOPLE

With my own hands, I have put a new shingle roof on my porch and installed a ceiling in my living room. But there was a time when I would have rather drunk muddy water than fool around with electricity. Changing a bulb was risky enough business for me. I would never have hung a light fixture. I couldn't even watch while one was being installed.

Once, when The Ex was putting in ceiling fans in the upper and lower hallways of our house, I couldn't watch. I was terrified that he would touch hot wires, put his hands in the wrong place, and 120 volts would charge through him and cut a path through to me, electrocuting us both when I spontaneously reached out to touch him. Our poor kids would be horrified when they arrived home from school to find themselves orphaned. Scrambling to shut off the main power switch was not the first thought that occurred to me. Neither did it occur to The Ex to shut the power off before handling the wires—a foolish omission that subtly established the Great Macho Divide, I suppose.

What remained as a memory resident program in my brain was "avoid electricity."

In most houses, if you mistakenly come in contact with live wires, you could get a surge that at worst could knock you off your feet, unless those feet were standing in water in which case you could be severely burned or even killed. However, the fail-safe design of circuit breakers and fuses is to shut down when there is an excessive surge of power, as would be the case when live wires touch or something, such as a human hand, interrupts the flow of current.

Although I still prefer to contract out the big electrical jobs, electricity no longer intimidates me. I've learned to understand it and to respect it. I've installed dimmer switches, plug-in receptacles (also called electrical outlets), and hung chandeliers and ceiling fans. Still, there are some electrical tasks better left to the utility company and folks who work with power for a living. A good rule of thumb is: Do not interfere with the power lines outside the house. But inside, anything from the service panel on is fair game.

These days there are a multitude of electrical chores I do myself and that you can do for yourself as well. Nonetheless, do not undertake a job without being equipped with a basic understanding of how power works. The good news is that it is not difficult to master.

Like most disciplines, the culture of electricity has a language of its own that keeps the uninitiated at a distance, creating a mystique that spawns "experts" who make their living interpreting the language and billing high costs for the translation and handling of the "dangerous" job. These mysteries are neither deep nor complicated, nor are they really mysteries, just unfamiliar territory for many of us. I intend to dispel the mystery. The information may seem an awful lot at first, but I offer it to you in bite-sized pieces. Consume it that way and eventually you will discover you have eaten the whole enchilada. And loved it.

Safety First

NEVER attempt an electrical task unless you are absolutely certain that you know what you are doing.

TURN OFF the power at the service panel (circuit breaker or fuse box) first thing. It is not enough to turn off the wall switch. The wall switch only interrupts current to the "hot" wire. You could still get a shock if you touch a neutral wire. If you are uncertain about which fuses or circuit breaker switches control the electrical outlet where you will be working, then disengage all of the house power by turning off the main power at the service panel.

TEST wires with a voltage tester before working on them.

MAKE SURE you are not standing on a wet floor.

BE AWARE of where your hands are and what is around you. You do not want to reach out for sudden support and touch bare metal such as pipes or ducts while working with electricity—you could make yourself an electrical conductor.

AVOID using a metal stepladder when doing electrical work for the same reason.

MATCH WIRES. Wires come in different sizes designed to handle varying degrees of electrical output. The larger the gauge of wire the more volts it can handle. Don't try to attach an 8-volt wire to one designed for 120 volts. It is like an 8-volt guy trying to make it with a 120-volt woman; early burnout is assured.

HAVE SOMEONE else present when you are working with electricity to ease the task, or to help you in the event of an emergency.

ALWAYS unplug an appliance before working on it.

EXAMINE appliances periodically and replace frayed cords and broken plugs.

Electrical Terms to Know

VOLTS OR VOLTAGE: Electricity, like water in a home's plumbing system, travels through the house wires under pressure. The force that moves the electricity through the wires is the volt or voltage.

AMPS, AMPERES, or AMPERAGE: The rate at which an appliance draws electricity is measured in amps.

WATTS or WATTAGE: The measure for the total amount of energy being consumed.

CURRENT: Flow of electricity.

AC: Alternating current is the standard electric power that services a residence or business. AC is distinguished by its reversal of direction at regular intervals of about sixty times a second. Think of alternating current as you making trips from your desk to the coffeemaker back to your desk, back to the coffeemaker, and back to your desk again at regular intervals during the day. You're the AC.

DC: Direct current flows in one direction. Batteries such as you'd find in radios or cordless tools are the source.

HOT WIRE: A wire live with electricity.

CIRCUIT BREAKERS AND FUSES: Interrupt the electrical circuit when it is overloaded. Circuit breakers must be reset once they have been tripped. Fuses must be replaced once they blow out.

FUSESTAT: Serves the same purpose as a fuse except that unlike a fuse it is reusable. Once it has been tripped it can be reset by pushing a little doodad that is attached to its front.

GROUNDING: Electrical charges in a home's electrical system can build to a dangerous level in a house if safeguards are not taken. The main safeguard is grounding, which in a literal sense means getting down to the ground. The electrical service in all homes must provide a safe path for electricity to the ground or else you would receive an electrical shock by touching anything, including each other. Code requires grounding for each circuit. Grounding is accomplished by installing copper wire in each switch and receptacle box in the home so that electrical charges are safely returned to the service panel. That task is usually done by an electrician at the time that the service is installed. From the service panel, a main grounding wire connects onto a metal water pipe. Current procedure under the National Electrical Code now requires one further safety step: A metal grounding rod is attached to the water pipe and buried in the earth at a minimum depth of eight feet. Hence the term "grounding" is quite literal.

How Electricity Works

ELECTRICAL SERVICE TO A THREE-STORY HOUSE

Your power company provides electricity to your neighborhood through overhead or underground cables that are connected to transformers. From the transformer, two 120-volt power cables transport electricity to a meter that measures the amount of electricity you use. You pay for what you use. The meter either is mounted on an outside wall of the house where the electric company meter reader can get to it when you are not home or, in older homes, mounted to a wall in the basement. The meter itself is wired to a service panel made up of either circuit breakers or fuses. Newer homes have circuit breakers. Older homes that have not had the electrical system upgraded usually have fuses.

Whether the service panel contains a circuit breaker or fuse system, it is connected to wires that snake through the walls of the house, connecting to the many switches and receptacle outlets that provide light and power.

Electrical Service to a House

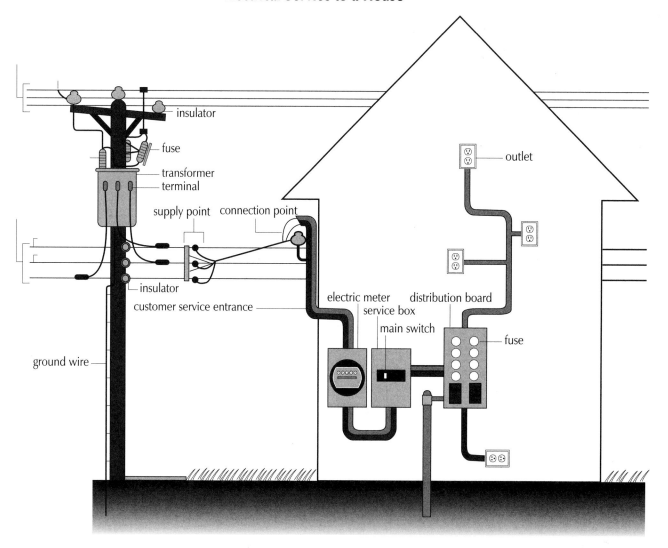

insulator

fuse

transformer
terminal

supply point   connection point

outlet

insulator

customer service entrance

electric meter
service box
main switch

distribution board

fuse

ground wire

POWER TO THE
PEOPLE

Reading the Meter

When the needle falls between two numbers, record the lower number.

With all of that electricity present, an electrical charge can built up in the system. Circuit breakers and fuses are the first line of defense against shock or an electrical fire when that happens. You could say that circuit breakers and fuses are the safety nets of a house's electrical system. Each circuit is protected by its own breaker or fuse and operates independently of the others. A tripped circuit breaker or blown fuse is telling you something is wrong. It could be that you have too many appliances hooked into one circuit, or a motor is being overworked, or bare wires are touching somewhere in a switch, fixture, or receptacle. Merely replacing the fuse or resetting the circuit breaker is *not* the answer. You must trace the trouble or the problem will recur until something really attention-getting happens, like a fire. The most common cause of power interruption is too many appliances hooked into the same circuit. Inadequate house power is another.

A cable carrying 120 volts of current into a house contains three wires—black, white, and a bare copper grounding wire (sometimes an insulated green wire). The black wire is the hot wire that delivers 120 volts to the circuit. The white wire, which is called neutral, returns the power to the source. The grounding wire provides an alternative path for electricity to return to the service panel.

A Little Applied History

Before 1941, homes had only 110/120 volts of electric service provided in a cable containing two wires. One wire carried the 120 volts to the house and the other wire provided the return to the source.

After 1941, houses were built with double the power, or 220/240 volts on a three-wire cable service. Translation: Power comes into the house on two wires—each carrying 110/120 volts—and leaves on the third wire. This may mean absolutely nothing to you right now, but to your amazement the static in your brain will ease as you become familiar with the concept and terms.

Understandably, the 220/240 system allows for the creation of more circuits to handle more power-demanding electrical appliances. Most appliances—toasters, microwave ovens, irons, and radios—can operate fine with only 120 volts of house power. However, when you add to the picture such modern-day heavy-duty creature-comfort and convenience appliances as your furnace, clothes dryer, refrigerator, or cooking range, you need to have the maximum voltage in the home. These heavy-duty appliances require far more juice to operate. And as a matter of safety, each of these appliances should have its own separate circuit.

**POWER TO THE
PEOPLE**

Anatomy of a Circuit

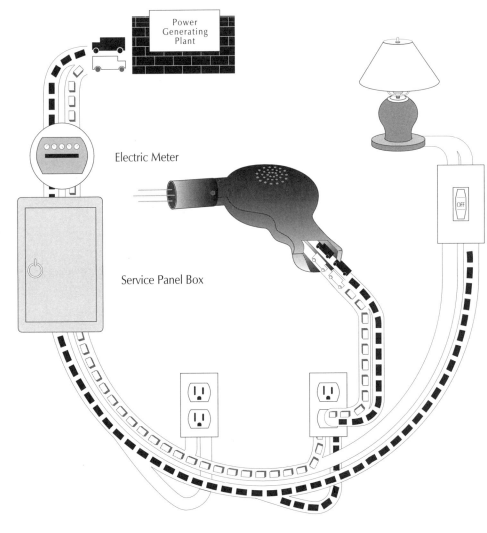

Power
Generating
Plant

Electric Meter

Service Panel Box

■ = hot wire
□ = neutral wire

► **TIP:**

Extension cords
everywhere? Lights flicker
when appliances are
turned on? A shrinking TV
picture? You may be
overloading a circuit.
Explore installing additional
circuits or redistributing the
ones you have.

Circuit Breaker Box

Circuit breakers operate independently of each other. When the power kicks off somewhere in the house, this is where to go to restore it. Look for the circuit breaker switch that displays a red bar in its panel or whose switch is in center position. To restart, flip the switch to the Off position then to On. Notice what rooms and appliances the circuit controls. That should be clearly marked next to each circuit switch. If after restoration the power kicks off again, there are either too many appliances and fixtures using the circuit (overload) or there's a short. A short could be caused by frayed or bare wires that are rubbing against each other in an appliance or electrical receptacle.

Solution: In the case of an overload, unplug one of the high-wattage appliances that's on the circuit, such as an iron. That should pinpoint the problem. If not, a short is a reasonable conclusion. To track down the source of the short, unplug all appliances connected to that circuit and systematically plug them back in, one at a time until the breaker trips.

If the circuit breakers are not already clearly identified, you should label each one with the names of the appliances or rooms they are supplying. This way you can quickly identify problem areas.

Labeling the Circuit Breakers

It will take two people to do this—one standing at the service panel and one roaming the house. The person at the service panel should notice that each circuit breaker or fuse has a number marked on it reading 15, 20, 30, 40, or 50. The numbers indicate the amount of amps that circuit handles. Circuits to most rooms are on 15 or 20 amps. The circuit breakers with the higher amp designation are for servicing heavy-duty appliances such as a furnace or a clothes dryer.

Circuit Breaker Box
with Main Disconnect

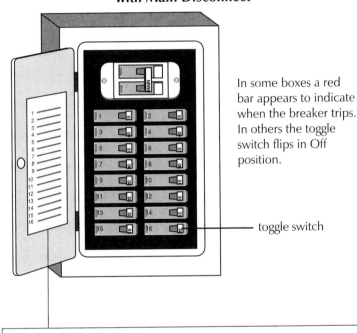

In some boxes a red bar appears to indicate when the breaker trips. In others the toggle switch flips in Off position.

toggle switch

Labeling your breakers

Amps	Breaker #	Area Serviced	Amps	Breaker #	Area Serviced
15	#1.	Powder Room	15	#2.	Bathroom Receptacles
40	#3. #5.	Range	40	#4. #6.	Air Conditioner
30	#7. #9.	Dryer	40	#8. #10.	Heating
20	#11.	Microwave	30	#12. #14.	Hot Water Heater
20	#13.	Kitchen Receptacles			
20	#15.	Washer	15	#16.	Dishwasher

The service panel person begins by turning off the house power not with the main switch but by individually flipping off each of the circuit breakers or unscrewing all of the fuses until the power is off everywhere. That done, the service panel person then flips one circuit breaker back on.

The roamer, who has prepared ahead of time by turning on at least one light switch or lamp in each room, finds the room or rooms where a light is on. They should turn on all light switches in the room and test receptacles by plugging a lamp in each. If one or more does not work, then either the receptacle or the switch is bad or it is powered by another circuit. The roamer should tape a note to the dead receptacle or switch to check later and let the service panel person know what room or rooms are controlled by the circuit that is on.

Meanwhile, the service panel person should label each circuit according to what the two of you discover that circuit controls: back bedroom, madam's boudoir, second-floor bathroom, and so on. Do this room by room, circuit by circuit. It will acquaint you with the electricity in the house.

Bedrooms typically are supplied by one 20-amp or two 15-amp circuits. Appliances typically found in the bedroom—lamps, a clock radio, and perhaps a compact stereo—have low wattage, which uses a small amount of amps. However, if there is a window air conditioner in the bedroom, it should be on its own circuit.

Now the kitchen is a different story. It typically utilizes high-wattage appliances and thus is supplied with electricity from two or more circuits. As a rule the dishwasher, garbage disposal, and microwave should be on separate circuits. If you turned on every appliance you have in the kitchen all at once, you would likely cause an overload. Naturally, the thinking behind the distribution of power in a kitchen, and any other room, is that all appliances and receptacles will not be in use at once so that the power supplied to the room should be sufficient. A good rule of thumb is any appliance or equipment with a heating element in it, such as an iron or toaster, should be on at least a 20-amp circuit.

What Watts Mean to You

POWER TO THE PEOPLE

The chart below shows the typical wattage (power) of familiar household appliances.

Appliance	Watts	Appliance	Watts	Appliance	Watts
Blender	200–400	Food mixer	250	Microwave oven	650
Clock radio	8	Fryer	1,600	Range (electric)	4,500
Coffeemaker	750	Furnace (gas) (240 volts)	800	Refrigerator	350
Clothes dryer (240 volts)	5,000–6,000	Furnace (oil) (240 volts)	1,200	Rotisserie	1,400
Clothes iron	1,000	Garbage disposal	500–1,000	Stereo	300–500
Curling iron	70	Hair blow dryer	400	Television (color)	200–4,500
Dishwasher	1,100	Space heater	1,000–1,500	Toaster oven	1,500
Freezer	300–600	Hot water heater	2,500–5,000		

How to Identify a Blown Fuse and Determine Cause

Good and Bad Fuses

Not all bad fuses look alike. The appearance of a blown fuse depends on what caused it to blow.

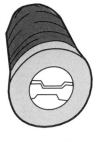

Good   Circuit overload   Short

Some Basic Electrical Tools

Tape measure, fuse puller, voltage tester, continuity tester, wire nuts, multipurpose wire stripper, needle-nose pliers, slot or flathead screwdriver, Phillips head screwdriver, utility knife, adjustable wrench, electric solder gun and solder.

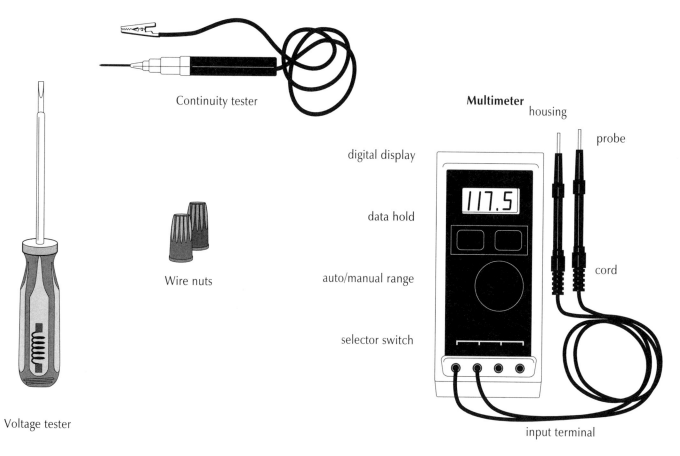

Continuity tester

Multimeter

housing

probe

digital display

data hold

cord

auto/manual range

selector switch

Wire nuts

input terminal

Voltage tester

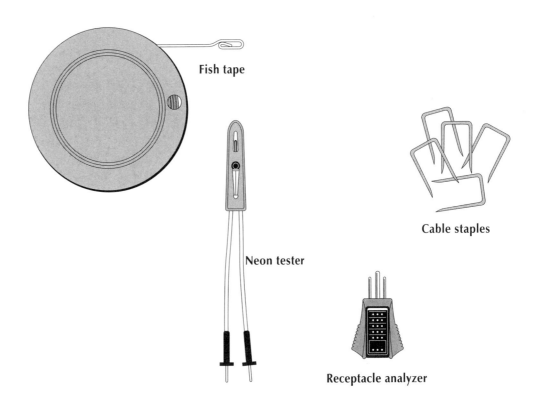

Fish tape

Neon tester

Cable staples

Receptacle analyzer

Switches, Receptacles, Fixtures, Cords, and Plugs

Troubleshooting and Repairing

One day, just for the heck of it, turn off the electrical power and remove a wall switch and a plug-in receptacle to see what it looks like in there. In fact, after you have read this section—assuming it is during a noncrisis

► ADVISORY!

Directions given are for
replacing existing devices,
not **installing** or creating a
switch and electrical outlet
where one did not
previously exist. Save the
creation for a licensed
electrician.

moment—take a practice run disconnecting and reconnecting these devices before a need arises. When the need does occur you will at least know what you are looking at. Familiarity is 80 percent of success.

Often, the first indication of an electrical problem is a fuse that blows constantly or a circuit breaker that frequently trips. A number of things could be triggering the outages: an overloaded circuit, a faulty appliance or lamp, or faulty wiring in an electrical receptacle box. Loose or damaged wires are common problems within receptacle boxes. Sometimes a wire will work itself free from a wire nut or terminal screw, thus breaking the flow of current to the receptacle or switch. Or a bare wire will touch the metal box or another bare wire and a short circuit will result.

When the problem has been traced to the receptacle, solutions might include reconnecting loose wires, repairing damaged wires or replacing the receptacle altogether.

Making the repairs really is a no-brainer. If you must replace a switch, receptacle, or a light fixture, pay close attention to the way the existing device is wired and reconnect the replacement device the same way. The wires usually are color coded. Usually. But there are exceptions.

Homes built before the 1950s were not subject to the uniform electrical code that requires color-coded wiring, so you may not find color-coded wiring on these older homes. However, that is not a problem. If you remove a switch, electrical outlet, or light fixture and find no color-coded wires, just carefully note how the existing device is connected before removing it. Mark the wires with masking tape or a color Magic Marker to guide you in connecting the replacement. You might write the code **top left screw (tls)** or **bottom left screw (bls)** on the marking tape you put on the wire to indicate which screw on the replacement switch, for example, gets attached to which wire.

WALL SWITCHES

There are three common residential switch types: a **single pole,** which controls a light from one location, a **three-way,** which operates a single light from two different locations, and a **four-way,** where controlling a single light from three or more locations is desired. There also is the power-saving **dimmer switch.**

Regardless of the switch you are replacing be certain that the new one has the identical amperage and voltage rating. The same goes for a receptacle. The rating usually is etched on the body of the device and would say, for example, **"15A-120 VAC Only."** Translation: The switch is good for up to 15 *a*mps of current at 120 *v*olts on an *a*lternating *c*urrent system.

To be certain that you get the right device, take the old one with you for comparisons. But **before** you disconnect the switch pay close attention to

Types of Switches

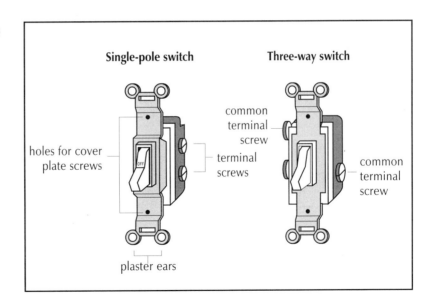

Single-pole switch

Three-way switch

holes for cover plate screws

common terminal screw

terminal screws

common terminal screw

plaster ears

which wires went where so that you hook up the replacement the same way as its predecessor. In the case of a three-way or four-way switch, marking the wires with pieces of masking tape will help you make the proper connections. For instance, with a three-way switch, you can mark the wires **LT (left top), LB (left bottom), RB (right bottom,** and **G (ground)** to correspond the wires to the proper screw terminals on the replacement switch.

A **voltage tester** will indicate if power is coming through a circuit you thought was turned off. It also is good for testing whether a receptacle is properly grounded. The tester consists of two insulated metal probes and a bulb and has no power of its own. The bulb will glow only if power is present. Some styles have two clips at the ends and some have thin metal probes. Hold the voltage tester by its rubber insulation only. Touch one of the probes to the metal box and touch the other probe to the screw terminal. If the electrical box is made of plastic, then touch one probe to the screw terminal and the other to the metal strap on the switch. If current is flowing, the tester bulb will glow. If the bulb glows, **Stop! Go and check the main power source again to be certain it is OFF.** That done, return to the switch and test it with the voltage tester once more. The bulb should not light up, indicating that the power is off.

REPLACING A SINGLE-POLE SWITCH

Tools needed: Screwdriver, needle-nose pliers, wire nuts, electrical tape, voltage tester, continuity tester.

1. **Turn off power** at the service panel.

2. Position the toggle switch to **OFF** and remove the switch plate by loosening the holding screws.

3. Use a voltage tester to double-check that the power to the switch outlet is off.

4. Gently pull the switch forward. Notice how the switch is wired. Label each wire with a small piece of masking tape.

5. Remove switch.

Replacing a Single-Pole Switch

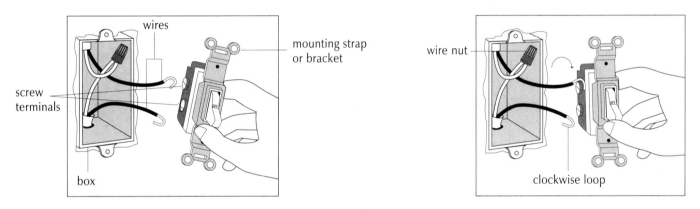

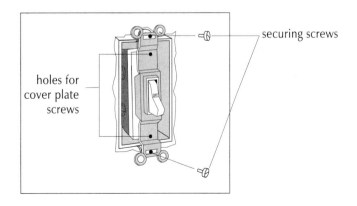

6. Check for damaged or loose wires. If the wire nut has worked itself loose, make sure that the wires are still firmly twisted together before screwing the nut back on. Reconnect a loose wire by looping its bare end around the terminal screw and tighten the screw.

7. Repair a broken wire by unhooking the damaged wire from the switch screw terminal. Snip off the damaged end and use a wire stripper to carefully peel back the insulation to expose some fresh wire. Take care not to gouge the wire. If the snipped wire is too short to reach the terminal screw, take a sample of the wire to the hardware store and ask for a piece of the same gauge. Strip the insulation back on both ends of the wire. Hook one end onto the switch terminal screw. Join the other end to the snipped wire, twist them together, and secure them with a wire nut.

8. If neither loose nor damaged wires are the problem, test the switch. Set the toggle to On. Attach the clip end of a continuity tester to one of the screw terminals and touch the probe end of the tester to the other screw terminal. Flip the toggle off, then on. If the switch is good, the tester will light only when the toggle is in the On position.

9. If the switch is bad, a replacement is needed. Take the old switch to the hardware store and buy a similar replacement.

10. With the toggle on the switch in the **OFF** position connect the wires to the screw terminals of the new switch.

11. When you have connected the replacement switch, gently push the wires into the box so that the switch fits snugly.

REPLACING A THREE-WAY SWITCH

Three-way switches exist in pairs. They are used to control a single light from two locations, such as a hall light with a switch control both upstairs and downstairs. If one of the switches fails to activate the light, you may need to test both.

Turn off the power. Begin testing the switch that appears to be giving you trouble. Follow the steps for troubleshooting the single-pole switch. If the first switch checks out all right, then repeat the routine with the other one.

Unlike the single-pole switch, the three-way switch has three terminals and is connected to three wires. All three wires are hot. Each wire is connected to a screw terminal. A fourth wire may be in evidence in newer homes. It is the ground wire and is bare copper. It should be hooked around the grounding screw that is on the switch. The grounding screw is recognizable because it generally is the smallest of the screws attached to the switch body and sometimes is painted green.

Replacing a Three-Way Switch

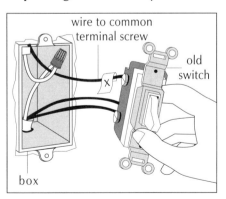

Before removing wires from terminal screws label one to be reconnected to top terminal screw of replacement switch. This will make it easy to see how to connect the remaining wires.

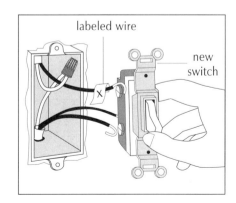

► **CAUTION!**

The total wattage controlled by the dimmer should not exceed the switch's rating, which is marked on the side of the switch. If it is rated for 600 watts maximum, for example, that's all the lighting that should be on that switch. Also, dimmer switches are not recommended for fluorescent lighting, as they can damage the lighting.

DIMMER SWITCHES

These switches are popular power savers and very easy to install. There are several kinds of dimmer switches: ones with a control knob, touch sensitive, and three-way. They fit inside standard electrical outlet boxes. Dimmer switches are not made with screw terminals. They have wires, usually two black ones on a single pole and two black and a red in the case of a three-way. Touch-sensitive dimmers have a black, red, and green wire.

Replacing or Installing a Programmable Timer Switch

There are several types of programmable timer switches ranging from "I dare you to figure me out" to "I'm easy." Timers are an inexpensive way of automatically providing security lighting inside or outside your home from dusk to dawn. You determine through programming when you want the front porch or backyard illuminated and with whatever regularity, within the feature limitations of the timer model selected. There's no point in selecting difficult when easy is available. Current models can replace any standard switch controlling indoor or outdoor incandescent lighting. What's more, it can be used with the existing wall switch plate. Always read the directions that come in the switch packaging first.

The timer switch is always a single pole.

1. **Turn off the power.**

2. Remove the switch plate.

3. Use a voltage tester to confirm that no current is coming through. Touch one probe of a voltage tester to the metal box and the other

probe to the bare end of each of the wires. The tester bulb should not glow. If it does, the power is still on. Return to the service panel and turn off the right circuit breaker or pull the proper fuse. To be sure, simply turn off the main switch.

4. Carefully note how the wires are connected to the existing timer switch. Wire the replacement switch exactly the same way. If you are replacing a regular switch with a timer, connect the wiring in the switch outlet to the wiring on the timer.

REPLACING A PLUG-IN RECEPTACLE

Duplex plug-in receptacles in most modern homes have screws that are called terminals. Generally, there are two silver-colored screws on one side, two brass-colored screws on the other, and a fifth, smaller screw that is sometimes painted green. This smaller screw is the ground terminal.

The receptacle is connected to power by hooking the bare end of the wires that are coming out of the receptacle box onto the brass and silver screw terminals. Some receptacles have holes on the back called "quick release" holes that eliminate the need to wrap wire around the screw terminals. To connect a "quick release" receptacle, gently push the end of the wires into the holes. The wires will automatically lock into place.

1. **Turn off power.**

2. Test both sockets of the receptacle with a voltage tester. (See illustration on page 44.)

3. Remove screw from cover plate and the screws holding the receptacle in the box.

4. Gently pull receptacle from the box.

5. Before loosening the wires, label them with masking tape—top silver (ts), lower silver (ls), top brass (tb), lower brass (lb), and (g) for the ground screw, which is painted green (g).

6. Loosen the terminal screws and free the wires.

7. Using your labeling as a guide, install the new receptacle, matching the wires with the corresponding terminal screw.

8. Gently push the wires into the box, reseat the receptacle, fasten it in place, and restore power.

9. Test both sockets of the receptacle with a receptacle tester to assure it is properly installed.

GROUND FAULT CIRCUIT INTERRUPTERS (GFCI)

These receptacles are specially designed to prevent shock. The National Electrical Code now requires these protective devices to be installed in all areas that are exposed to moisture such as the kitchen, bathrooms, laundry rooms, workshops, garages, patios, poolside, and so forth. The GFCI automatically grounds appliances that are plugged into it. It trips, or interrupts power instantly when it detects the slightest interruption in current, which could be caused by the presence of moisture, damaged wiring, or a faulty appliance. It is a terrific outlet for old houses where grounding in electrical boxes and receptacles was not routinely done. In fact, even with new construction proper grounding could be absent, especially where electricians are overly concerned about time and money.

The GFCI should be checked periodically to ensure proper functioning. This is done by pressing the button marked **TEST.** When the test button is pressed, the reset button should pop out. If it does not, the outlet should be checked for loose wires or a bad receptacle.

Types of Receptacles

Duplex Receptacle

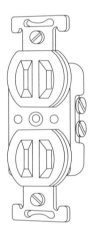

Hi-Voltage Receptacle

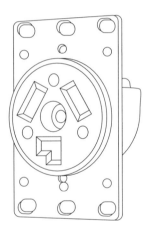

Middle-of-the-Run GFCI
(Ground Fault Circuit Interrupter)

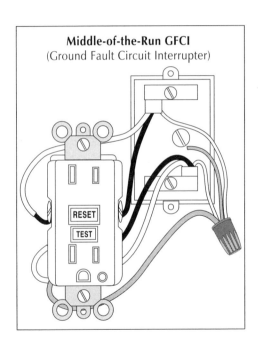

RESET

TEST

Ceiling Fan

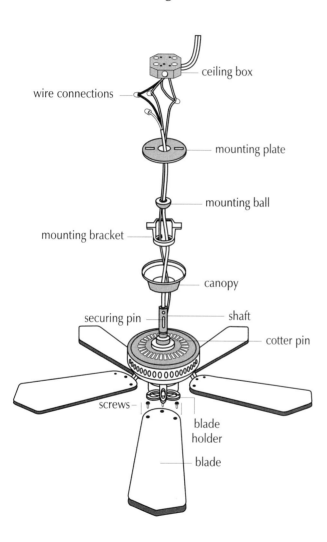

ceiling box

wire connections

mounting plate

mounting ball

mounting bracket

canopy

securing pin — shaft

cotter pin

screws

blade holder

blade

REPLACING A CEILING LIGHT OR FAN

First, get a work partner. Working overhead is awkward. You will need someone to help handle the light fixture.

Turn off the power at service panel, then unfasten the light fixture canopy. Notice how the fixture is fastened to the ceiling. It may be secured with a metal strap and screws or it may be held by a **hickey** that screws onto a threaded stud that protrudes from the center of the electrical box.

What you might see up there. With the canopy unfastened there are a few scenarios you could encounter. There may be five wires coming from the ceiling. All may be in colors—black, white, green, red, and copper—and maybe not. There may be just two wires both wrapped in black electrical tape as is typical in older houses where wiring has not been updated. There may be a black and a white wire or two white wires, one of which has black tape on the end. In any case, there are only two wires coming from the ceiling that you should be concerned with and they already are connected to the existing fixture.

Preassemble the replacement light fixture. It should have three wires or leads (pronounced "leeds")—a copper ground wire and two others. Sometimes one of the others is black and the other is white and sometimes they are the same color.

If the ends of the wires are not bare, strip away approximately a one-inch length of plastic from the end of each to expose the wire. Join the fixture wires to those coming from the ceiling by twisting their ends together. Secure with wire nuts that are screwed onto the wire ends.

LAMPS AND EXTENSION CORDS

The lamp won't work and the bulb is good. Wait! Don't throw out the lamp. Rewire it! Cords, plugs, and sockets do wear out over time, and changing them is a simple matter. Some people opt to splice a worn-out lamp cord. Don't. It is not a safe option. Replace the cord altogether.

Extension cords are a temporary, not permanent, part of electrical service. If at all possible, appliances should be plugged directly into the electrical outlet. But when the occasion calls for an extension, choose wisely.

Not all extension cords are suitable for all usages. The wire in the cord has to be able to conduct sufficient current to the appliance. If the cord wire is too thin, it can overheat and possibly catch fire.

Longer is not necessarily better. A too long, thin cord can waste power, as the voltage has to travel farther than is necessary, weakening by the time it arrives at the appliance. A voltage loss of about 2 percent is typical, but a consistently higher voltage loss can burn out an element or weaken a motor.

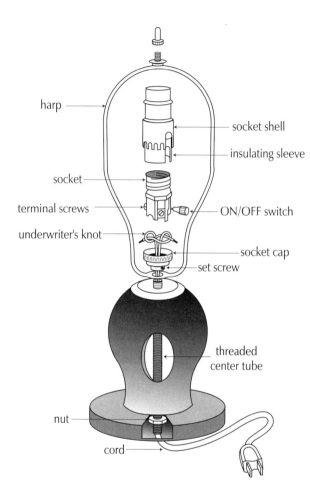

harp

socket shell

insulating sleeve

socket

terminal screws

ON/OFF switch

underwriter's knot

socket cap

set screw

threaded
center tube

nut

cord

A heavy-duty extension cord should be used for large watt-drawing appliances such as an air conditioner, power tools, or appliances with a heating element in them. When selecting an extension cord, check the notations on usage.

Parts of a Lamp

DOORBELLS AND CHIMES

A doorbell system is simple. It consists of three essential parts: a bell or chime, a push button or switch to activate the bell at the rear, side, or back of the house, and a transformer.

Doorbells, chimes, intercoms, and some accent lighting require only a low 8 to 15 volts to operate. Most doorbell systems are wired through the house current, which at 120 volts is a good deal stronger than what the doorbell needs. That's where the transformer comes in. Its job is to "step down," or reduce, the house's 120 volts of current to about 8 to 15 volts by the time it reaches the bell. The transformer can be found attached to a junction box somewhere near the service panel or in the case of my house on a junction box in the basement attached to a ceiling beam that is no where near the service panel.

Figuring out why a doorbell or chime won't ring, won't stop ringing, or rings with a whimper is done through the process of elimination. The problem could be a worn-out push button, dirty or moist contacts, a loose wire connection on the bell or chimes, a loose wire connection on the transformer, a bad transformer, or faulty house wiring.

Ding Dong the Bell Won't Ring

If the bell or chime doesn't ring at all, go to the main service panel and check for a tripped circuit breaker or blown fuse. While you are there check the transformer for loose wire connections. Next, remove the cover of the chimes or doorbell and check for loose wire connections.

Testing the Push Button

The contacts of a doorbell push button or switch that is exposed to weather can corrode and can affect the bell's performance. Some push buttons are surface-mounted or recessed in the doorframe or wall. They are easy to remove with a screwdriver.

Testing the Push-Button Switch

Turn off the power by tripping the circuit breaker or removing the fuse that services the bell. Go to the doorframe and remove the push-button switch cover. Clean the contacts by gently rubbing them with fine sandpaper. Pry up the contacts slightly with a screwdriver. Replace the cover. Turn on the power and push the button. If the bell won't stop ringing, the contacts are bent too far up. Turn off the power, remove the button, and adjust the contacts.

If the bell or chime won't ring at all, unscrew the push-button mounting plate from the doorframe or wall. Pull it forward to expose the wires. Unhook the wires from the terminal screws. Check for breaks in the wire. Snip off damaged ends and strip the insulation back to expose a fresh length of wire. Disconnect the wires from the terminal screws and twist them together. Turn on the power. If the chime or bell rings the push-button is bad.

Replacing the Push-Button

Turn off the power by tripping the circuit breaker or removing the fuse that controls service to the bell. Remove the old push button and mounting plate and disconnect the wires. Reconnect the wires to the terminal screws of the new mounting place.

REPLACING A DOORBELL CHIME

Most chime assemblies have three terminals marked FRONT, TRANS, and REAR that are connected to the FRONT door push button, the TRANSformer, and the REAR push button. Bell-type assemblies generally have only two terminals that connect to the front door push button and the transformer.

Turn off the power to the circuit controlling the doorbell. Before disconnecting the wires, use masking tape to label each wire FRONT, TRAN, REAR.

Loosen the terminal screws, remove the wires, and unscrew the chime from the wall. Purchase a replacement unit that uses the same voltage.

Thread the wires through the opening in the back of the replacement unit and screw it to the wall. Hook each of the labeled wires to their corre-

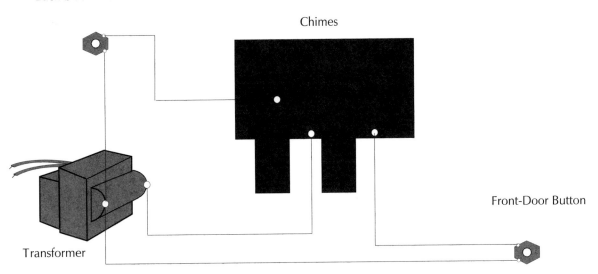

Back-Door Button

Chimes

Transformer

Front-Door Button

sponding terminal screw and tighten the screw. Install the face cover on the chime and turn on the power.

Testing the Transformer

Check the transformer for any loose wires at the low voltage (output) terminals. Turn off the power and tighten the connections. Turn on the power. If the chime or bell still doesn't work, the problem may be either a bad transformer or faulty input wiring leading from the main panel to the transformer.

Remove the transformer cover. Test the input wires by simultaneously touching the probes of a voltage tester to the terminal screws that have the black and white wire connected to them. If the tester bulb does not light, there is no power going to the transformer from the house wiring. You'll need an electrician to check the 120-volt wiring.

If a new transformer is needed, be sure to replace it with one that has the same voltage as that marked on the old one.

REPLACING THE TRANSFORMER

Turn off the power. Disconnect the wires on the low-voltage side of the transformer that connect to the bell. Next, disconnect the transformer wires in the junction box. Unscrew the transformer from the junction box. Buy a replacement with the same voltage and amperage rating.

Feed the two wires of the new transformer through the junction box. Twist one transformer wire to the black wire and one to the white wire. Secure the ends with a wire nut. Screw the transformer to the junction box. Connect the bell wires to the low-voltage transformer terminal screws. Turn on the power.

**POWER TO THE
PEOPLE**

Step-Saving Alternative for Troubleshooting a Faulty Bell

Because a doorbell operates on very low power—from 8 to 15 volts—a problem with it can be safely checked *without* turning off the power. One alternative method of testing the cause of a troublesome bell is to remove the push button and mounting plate, turn it over, and place a screwdriver across the terminals. If the bell rings, the button is bad and should be replaced. If the bell doesn't ring, remove the wires from the terminal screw and touch them together. If the bell rings, the problem is with the whole push-button switch assembly. If it does not ring the problem may be a loose connection on the chime or with the transformer or a tripped circuit breaker.

Turn off the power before working on the chime or transformer.

► REAL MAN
TIP:

By all means, show him your circuit breakers but reveal them only one circuit at a time.

4

PLUMB OUT OF YOUR MIND

Pipe Dreams

A visit from the plumber is never cheap. That's why we learn to live with the toilet that keeps running long after we've flushed it and the leaky faucet that has dripped so long that a brown stream stains the white enamel sink bowl. It is why we've conditioned ourselves to no longer jump when the pipes make that distracting bang after we turn off the water in the powder room and why we put up with a host of other plumbing breakdowns until they become full-blown emergencies and we have to call the plumber.

But we really don't have to hold ourselves hostage to either bad plumbing or plumbers' fees. Most plumbing repairs are simple enough for garden-variety folks like us to do ourselves. In fact, professional plumbers would prefer that we do the common stuff and save the really big jobs for them.

The first and only house The Ex and I bought together was at least fifty years old. At that age, a house is halfway through its life cycle. The first half century of a house's life is spent working the bugs out. The second half could be very rewarding if the owners pay attention to the maintenance signals.

Our house had all of the original plumbing throughout, which consisted of heavy, once-gray galvanized pipes. The insides of the pipes were encrusted with a half century of rust that made a one-inch water pipe function like a swizzle stick. As new homeowners, we didn't have a nickel to pay anybody to do anything.

Like a beautiful day, the poverty that comes with new homeownership makes you think you have talents you really don't possess. Thus, we decided to tackle the plumbing ourselves. We pulled out most of the old stuff singlehandedly and replaced it with a new kind of plastic PVC (polyvinyl chloride) piping that plumbers were pushing back then. The pipes locked together with a plastic ring nut and pipe glue, making them a breeze to work with.

Handling the job was easy as long as we stayed in the basement where we could see everything. Blindly fishing the pipes up through the walls to connect to the fixtures on the first and second floors was impossible. We didn't know what the heck we were doing. After a few days of failed improvising, children complaining, and communal birdbaths at the spigot in the basement, we gave in and called a plumber to finish the job.

A dozen years later I was faced with replacing that plumbing that was supposed to last a lifetime. For about a week I had been performing triage on one length of the plastic cold water pipe, which was springing a leak every six inches. That's when I learned that the particular type of plastic we installed had never passed the housing codes of a lot of cities, including ours, because of the very problem I was experiencing. "But," you say, "plumbers recommended it, so it must have been good."

Well, no. The important thing to know about plumbing right after remembering to turn off the water at the main valve before working on a water pipe, is: A plumber who works in a plumbing store is there because he has something to sell; thus, he is a salesman first and foremost. His assurances are suspect, particularly with a new product. 'Tis a pity we don't have the clarity of hindsight up front. Let my experience serve as your up-front hindsight.

Nonetheless, back to my story. I decided to have all of the plastic plumbing in the house replaced with copper, which has proven over time to be a more durable material. I figured out what needed to be done, priced the material, and hired for the job a licensed plumber who fit into my price range and came highly recommended by a friend who had used his services.

He was impressively efficient, a spare fellow with focused eyes, a utilitarian manner, and small patience for jawboning. He arrived as promised at 7:00 A.M. sharp, said good morning, announced what he was going to do, and commenced working. My kind of guy. Seven hours later, with no lunch break, he was done. I was happy to know he didn't have to come back the next day, but I was also a little edgy for no solid reason. New plumbing will do that to you.

That first night I had a nightmare that the water pressure forced the new copper pipes apart at the joints and flooded the house. In the dream I was awakened by the sound of rushing water to discover my bed floating out of the room and down the stairs. The house was engulfed in water. I scrambled toward the head of the bed in a panic and made a desperate grab for the headboard, but it remained out of reach by a fingertip. Suddenly a great wave crested above me, forcing a desperate scream from my throat. I woke up. It was just a bad dream. I checked the pipes. Everything was intact.

However, it was a different story by the time I got home from work later that evening. The nightmare sound of rushing water in the basement greeted me at the door. In the basement the water was about ankle deep, which meant the hot water heater, which was staged on a six-inch block of cement, was in imminent danger since its heating element was located at its bottom.

I grabbed my rubber boots from nearby and waded through to the main water cutoff. An important digression: (1) If you own a house, own a pair of at least ankle-high rubber boots. (2) Flooding and fire emergencies tend to bring the fire department to mind. However, **DO NOT** bring them to the house. Yes, you are experiencing an emergency but it is one *you* must be prepared to handle yourself. A wet/dry shop vacuum should be standard equipment at home.

Back to the story. With the water now cut off I telephoned the efficient plumber. He said he was unable to come out until the next morning. I was left to my own devices. I called a friend and got out a borrowed shop vac and a rag mop. As I dried up the basement, trying mightily to tolerate my helper's unsympathetic, lame water jokes, I kept thinking about the drain I'd been advised more than once to install for emergencies just as this. In fact the same person suggested that I replace my old shop vac. I did neither. A drain certainly would have kept the water level down to a minimum.

When the efficient plumber arrived the next morning, he was apologetic though not so contrite as to refund my money. The problem was that he'd "forgotten to sweat a joint." Plumber talk can be so poetic. In other words, he failed to permanently seal two pipes, which is done by melting soldering iron onto the pipes at the coupling ring where they are joined. The solder, which is softened with the flame from a butane torch, hardens quickly as it cools. It was a mistake you would not expect a professional to make. Still, to err is human and it happened. Despite the problem, contracting out to a professional a job as major as this one was the smart thing to do. Besides the fact that he knew what he was doing and therefore could do it quickly, it provided an essential element for when things go wrong: Someone else to blame!

Coming and Going

Humanity has learned how to harness the enormous power of water to supply electricity and water service to our homes. It is especially humbling to note that the water supplied to homes by private or public systems all originates as rainfall. Rainwater is collected in a variety of ways in lakes, rivers, reservoirs, cisterns, underground wells, or springs. Utility companies have figured out how to use gushing pressure to supply water to a home plumbing system.

A home's plumbing system is simple. It involves two sets of pipes—incoming and outgoing. Fresh-water pipes supply hot and cold service. Drains take water and solid wastes from the fixtures and to sewage pipes, which ferry the waste away from the house and into the public sewage or a private septic tank. There are at least three hundred feet of supply lines and waste pipes concealed under floors and in the walls in the average house.

Fresh or potable water supply is pumped into the house under pressure and carried by copper or plastic pipes to the various plumbing fixtures in the bathrooms, kitchen, and laundry room. The water supply splits up at the water heater, dividing into pipes carrying hot water and cold water. Water from a private system goes to a pressure tank before going to the heater.

Gases

The outgoing drainage pipes use gravity to shuttle solid waste and liquids away from the various fixtures—the toilets, sinks, shower, and so forth—and into the sewer system. Drainage pipes also provide the venting that keeps a balance of pressure inside the pipes to prevent foul-smelling gases from building there. You would never think it, but a vital part of the vent-

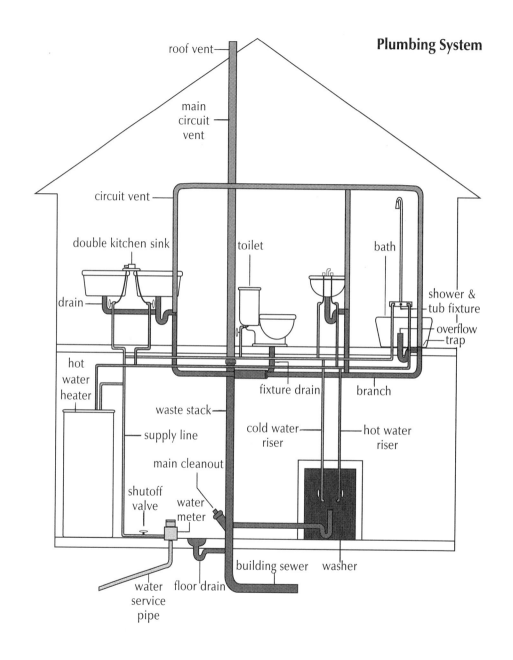

Plumbing System

roof vent

main
circuit
vent

circuit vent

double kitchen sink

drain

toilet

bath

shower &
tub fixture

overflow
trap

fixture drain

branch

hot
water
heater

waste stack

cold water
riser

hot water
riser

supply line

main cleanout

shutoff
valve

water
meter

building sewer

washer

water
service
pipe

floor drain

ing system for house plumbing is on the roof. The pipe sticking up visibly through the roof is the plumbing's ventilation.

DWV

Fresh-water pipes are notably smaller than drainage pipes, measuring one to one and a quarter inches around, while the diameter of drainage pipes is four inches. The drainage system is often referred to as the DWV system. That's shorthand for drain, waste, vent, that is, the drain pipe.

Traps

You will notice under your sinks a U- or S-shaped pipe. This bend in the pipe is called a **trap** and is an essential part of the venting system. Traps also exist under the toilet but are hidden under the flooring. The bend holds a small amount of water, which acts as a seal to trap or block gases and bacteria that build up in the pipes from waste material. Without the trap the house would smell like the sewer. The water that sits in the toilet bowl is another gas barrier. It not only serves to carry away wastes but to block sewage gases from entering the house.

Help!!!

Emergencies happen. The first thing to do is not panic. Most modern plumbing systems provide shutoff valves at the sink, toilet, laundry appliances, and on every pipe transporting fresh water, making it possible to shut off a problem area without affecting the rest of the water service. The valves usually are located in plain view beneath, or somewhere in very close proximity to, the fixtures they are supplying. If a shutoff valve is not easily accessible at the fixture or appliance, turn off the main water supply valve in the basement of the house or at the water heater, in the case of a condominium. (In an apartment building the main utility cutoff generally is in the basement and probably off-limits to the tenants. You'll have to wait on the landlord or maintenance personnel.) If the problem in your home is that a water pipe has sprung a leak, turn off the main shutoff. If you are uncertain of where the master shutoff valve is, go to the water meter and follow the pipes to where they leave the house. The master valve should be somewhere nearby.

Without the right tools simple jobs become difficult. While you may have an adequate collection of basic hand tools you probably won't have just the right ones for the plumbing task when you need them. But that's all right. Eventually, you will. If you're lucky, you won't. However, if your luck gives way, as it is likely to do if you live indoors, you will want to have the right tools at hand.

There are about twenty basic tools and a handful of materials necessary for working with plumbing. Some of the tools might seem redundant but are not. For example, a pipe wrench and a monkey wrench. Close inspection reveals that the monkey wrench has smooth jaws, which you would want to use to avoid scarring the surface of a decorative nut. The pipe wrench has jaws with ridges.

An auger is used to clear stoppages in the pipes. But there is a **drain auger** for clearing drains and traps and a **closet auger** especially designed for clearing traps in toilets.

You may already have on hand Allen wrenches, a couple of screwdrivers, and rib joint pliers, but you also might need a **valve seat wrench** for removing really worn-out faucet seats. The long, slender **basin wrench** is excellent in impossibly tight spaces for loosening or tightening the faucet's retaining bolts located under the sink on the backside.

Besides tools, certain materials are needed for sealing two pipes to-

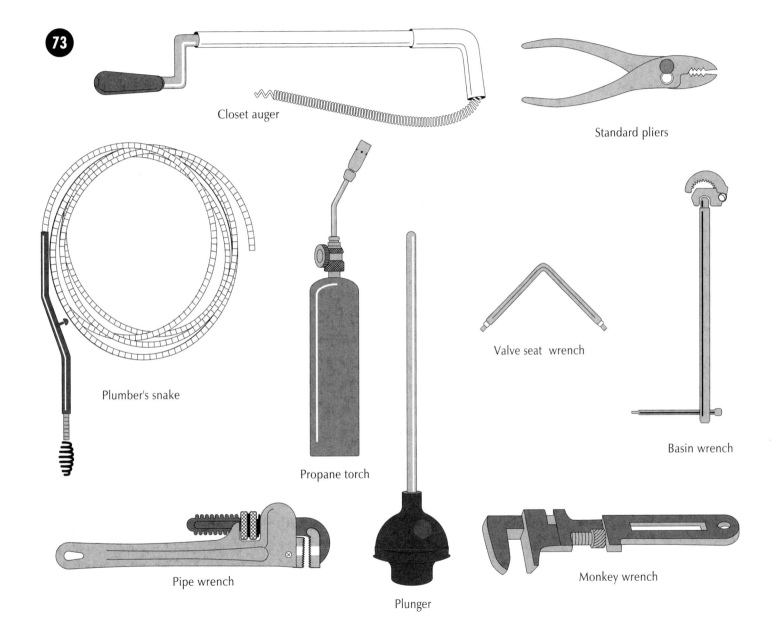

73

Closet auger

Standard pliers

Plumber's snake

Propane torch

Valve seat wrench

Basin wrench

Pipe wrench

Plunger

Monkey wrench

gether. Because even the thinnest layer of oil or dirt will prevent an adhesive from bonding properly, you will need to rub the tips of the pipes with fine **sandpaper** or **emery cloth** to clean the areas to be joined. Applying **flux,** a substance used to clean the pipe surface, will allow solder to flow freely and aid the bonding process. Joining two pipes, or "sweatin' da joints," calls for melting **plumbers' solder,** which looks like thin gray wire, onto the prepared pipe ends with a **propane torch. Solvent cement** is an adhesive used for joining plastic pipes and **joint sealing tape** and **pipe joint compound** work well for temporary pipe repairs.

Changing and/or Repairing a Faucet

DRIP, DRIP, DRIP

There are several types of faucets, all of which can leak after a time from a variety of places because of normal wear. Generally, the problem can be pinpointed to one of two reasons: worn-out washers that no longer fit the valve seat or string packing around the stem that has deteriorated from the routine of turning the valves to Off and On positions. Washers and string packing are what restrain the flow of water from the stem when the valve is open.

A dripping spout usually signals a worn washer, worn seat, or both. Leaking around the handle generally indicates worn packing, although not all faucets have washers and packing. Newer faucets are washerless with a more durable diaphragm or rubber seal assembly. Some have plastic cartridges. Older faucets have a rope or string packing around the stem to prevent leakage. Nonetheless, old or new, parts break down and replacing them is not difficult.

For starters, you will need an assortment of washers, plumber's packing rope, O-rings, small brass screws, plumber's putty, and plumbing tools. When the time arrives you might decide it is easier to install a new faucet rather than repair the old, and in many cases that's true. But don't mistake your fear of doing the task for pragmatism.

Be not discouraged if you disassemble the faucet, replace parts, put them all back together, and the darned thing still leaks. Take it apart again and be certain the screws and nuts are tight, though not too tight, and the washers are properly seated. It sometimes takes even professional plumbers more than one attempt to get the job right. Just take your time and remember that women have in abundance what only a few men possess—finesse and patience. These two are a critical pair of assets when working with the trial and error of manipulating a multitude of tiny objects and often are even more important to getting the job done than prior knowledge.

MAKING THE REPAIRS—ALL MODELS

Step 1. Turn off the water supply to the fixture either at the valves under the sink or at the main water supply.

Step 2. Drain the lines by fully opening the hot and cold water faucets after turning off the water supply.

Step 3. Take note of the type of faucet you have.

Step 4. Begin disassembling the faucet.

Step 5. Slowly remove each of the parts, noticing the order of the inner assembly. Using the diagrams as a guide, identify the type of faucet it is.

LEAKING AROUND THE HANDLE

Tightening the stem nut should stop a leak at the base of the faucet. If not, the seal around the stem needs to be replaced. Depending on the age of your faucet, the seal could be one of three types: a ropelike material called packing that is wrapped around the top of the stem, a packing washer that fits inside the stem retaining nut, or one or more small O-rings that fit into grooves in the stem.

If the stem uses O-rings, coat them with a thin application of petroleum jelly before putting them on the stem to reduce friction. Gently clear away any corrosive deposits on the stem using fine steel wool. Put the faucet back together and turn on the water. If there is a clatter, the washer is loose. Turn off the water and undo the faucet once more, removing the stem to tighten the screw on the washer a bit more. If the problem is that water seeps out from around the handle, then the nut that holds the stem in place may not be tight enough. Remove the handle and give the nut another quarter turn.

ROTATING BALL-TYPE ONE-HANDLE

Patience, patience, patience. This is one of the most vexing faucets when it comes to repairs. It is virtually impossible to pinpoint the cause of the leak. You think you've fixed the problem only to see it show up again a few days later. Personally, I would drop-kick it through the goalpost of life and get a more cooperative style. In fact, that is what I did. But that's impetuous and not always fiscally practical.

Even the manufacturer knows the faucet is a pain and thus sells repair kits that contain all of the parts and a special wrench to work with called a tension-ring spanner. The best bet for saving yourself time and high blood pressure with this model is to replace all of the parts.

Stem Faucet

handle

packing nut

packing

washer

spindle

stem holder

stem washer

spout

thread

valve seat

Ball Type Faucet

handle

spout
aerator

bonnet

body

packing retainer ring

washer

ball assembly

valve seat

spring

O-ring

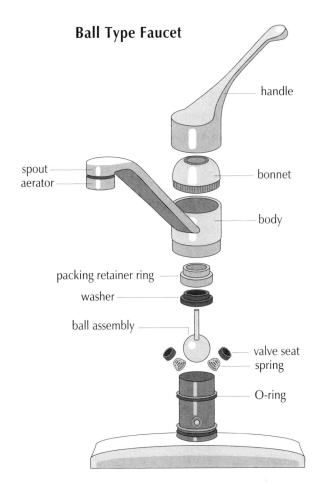

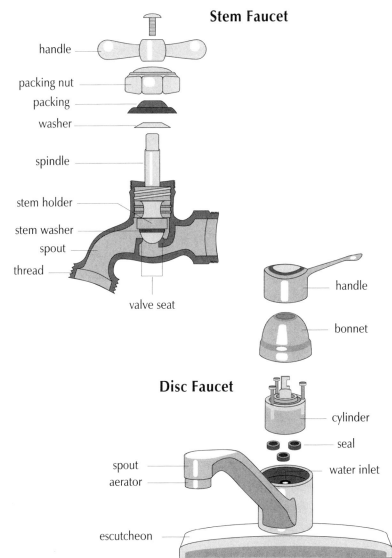

handle

bonnet

Disc Faucet

cylinder

seal

spout
aerator

water inlet

escutcheon

Take the faucet apart by first removing the handle with a screwdriver or Allen wrench. Many times a leak is caused by a loose tension ring, which is a notched, threaded piece. Tighten it with the tension-ring spanner wrench, which is designed to fit into the notches. Put the faucet back together and turn on the water to see if the leak is fixed. If it isn't, turn the water off and disassemble the faucet removing the handle, tension ring, cam, gasket, ball, seals, and springs. Install the new parts in the reverse order that you removed the old parts.

ONE-HANDLE CARTRIDGE STYLE

The fastener securing the cartridge in this style faucet often is difficult to detect. There's a cartridge-retaining clip, which is either on the inside under the handle or on the outside of the faucet. Carefully examine the outside of the faucet body below the handle, checking for a little ridge projecting out of the body. If you feel or see one, it is probably the retaining clip. Pull the clip out with a pair of pliers or a screwdriver. Then lift the handle and cartridge out of the faucet. Take the handle off and you will see the cartridge. Remove the retainer ring at the base of the cartridge to get to the retaining clip. Pull the clip out and then remove the cartridge. Take the cartridge to a plumbing supply store and get a replacement. That should solve the problem.

The hardest part about completely replacing a faucet is fitting your body into the tight quarters beneath and at the backside of the sink. A basin wrench with its long slim handle and slender jaws will come in handy. First, notice the kind of water supply pipes you have: plastic, copper tubing, or threaded. That will determine whether the pipe connection will be accomplished with solvent cement, solder, compression, or flare fittings.

Cartridge Faucet

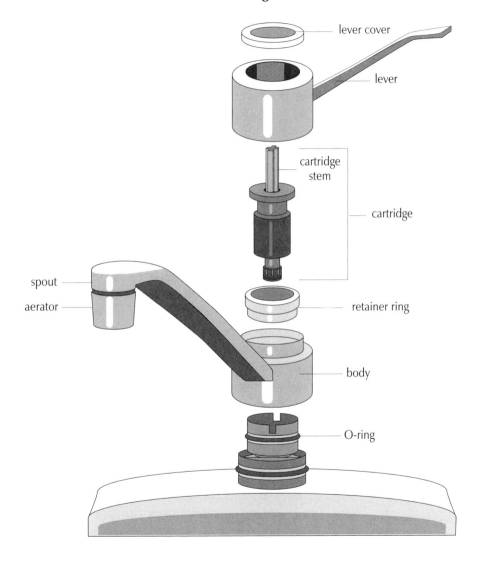

lever cover

lever

cartridge
stem

cartridge

spout

aerator

retainer ring

body

O-ring

Repairing the Spray Hose

Once, I completely unhooked the spray hose from my kitchen sink with the intention of discarding it because I thought it was beyond repair. The sprayer would spit like a teething two-year-old when I turned on the faucet. A little calm-headed investigation revealed a simple solution to the common problem of low water pressure at the nozzle that my spray hose was experiencing.

Check the spray head for clogging and then check the hose for kinks. By hand, unscrew the spray head nozzle. Then turn on a faucet and press the spray handle to flush deposits from the interior of the head. If the head is cracked replace it. Check the hose for serious kinks. If there are any, try smoothing or twisting them out with your hands. If that does not work, be sure the faucet is turned off and remove the spray hose by loosening the hex nut connection below the faucet under the sink. Buy a replacement hose.

Sinks and Tubs

Don't reach for the Drāno or any other chemical drain declogger if a drain is completely backed up. If the chemical happens not to work right away and you decide to try the plunger, you expose yourself to the splashback of dangerous caustic water. On a rare occasion, plumbing will clog at the main drain. However, generally, a clogged drain is isolated to one sink or fixture. Just removing the stoppers and strainers in a sink or tub and clearing the hair and other debris trapped on them may be all that is necessary.

If that's not enough though, there are a few nontoxic solutions. A device called a Drain Blaster is very efficient. It is patterned after equipment

**PLUMB OUT OF
YOUR MIND**

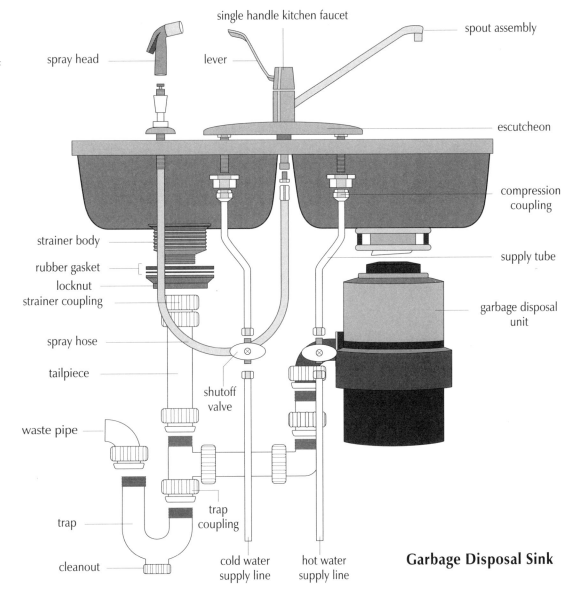

single handle kitchen faucet

spray head

lever

spout assembly

escutcheon

compression
coupling

strainer body

rubber gasket

locknut

strainer coupling

supply tube

garbage disposal
unit

spray hose

tailpiece

waste pipe

shutoff
valve

trap

trap
coupling

cleanout

cold water
supply line

hot water
supply line

Garbage Disposal Sink

Tub/Shower Assembly

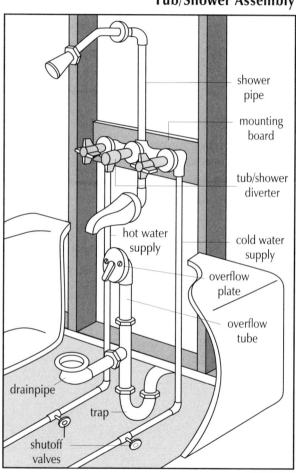

shower
pipe

mounting
board

tub/shower
diverter

cold water
supply

overflow
plate

overflow
tube

hot water
supply

drainpipe

trap

shutoff
valves

used by municipalities to clear clogged main drains. The home design uses tap water funneled through a thin rubber hose that pushes through the clog in sinks, tubs, and toilets.

An old-fashioned plunger can also be used to blast out obstructions. (However, remember: Don't use it if you've recently poured a chemical declogger in the drain.) Smear a little Vaseline around the rim of the plunger for a tighter seal around the drain. Running just enough water in the bowl or tub to cover the mouth of the plunger increases the seal. Work the plunger by rapidly pushing the stick handle up and down without breaking the contact between the plunger and the mouth of the drain. In the case of bathroom sinks, tubs, or showers, plug up the overflow hole with a rag to help build pressure as you plunge. With bathtubs and showers remove the pop-up stopper before plunging.

If plunging fails, insert an auger (commonly called a snake) in the drain and crank the handle until the spring cord breaks though the blockage. With bathtubs, if only a few inches of the auger will go into the drain and the stoppage is not clear, the problem may be the trap below the overflow. You can get to the tub trap through the overflow device. Remove the overflow by unscrewing the plate and pulling out all of the parts that include the pop-up or trip lever assembly. They should all be linked to each other, and gentle maneuvering should remove the whole thing at once. Feed the auger through the overflow into the trap until the blockage is cleared. That should do it.

Toilets

You can look at the water level in a toilet bowl and sense when there is a clogging problem. It would either be unusually high or low. At a time like that resist the temptation to flush, as you'll be courting a flood. Using a cup and sponge begin by baling out whatever water is in the toilet. Insert a small mirror partway into the toilet drain and pointing a flashlight inside see if you can spot any obstruction at the top of the trap. If you do, use a wire coat hanger to fish it out. If that is not the case, the next step is to plunge. In order for the plunger to work effectively it should fit in a tight seal around the toilet drain. The bowl should be half full, so use a bucket and add some water. Vigorously work the plunger handle up and down about a dozen times, then abruptly pull it away. If the water drains and you hear a gurgling sound, the line is cleared. Check by pouring in a bucket of water. If that goes down well, pour another bucket of water in for good measure.

Say that none of that works. Then it's closet auger time. This type of tool has a longer handle than the trap and drain version. A closet auger will grind through any obstruction except a solid object. You operate it by pulling the spring up to the handle, placing the coiled end well into the toilet outlet, and cranking the handle. If it feels as if you hit something solid or something is rattling around in the toilet, you'll have to unbolt the toilet bowl, turn it upside down, and try to shake or poke whatever is in there out. Sorry.

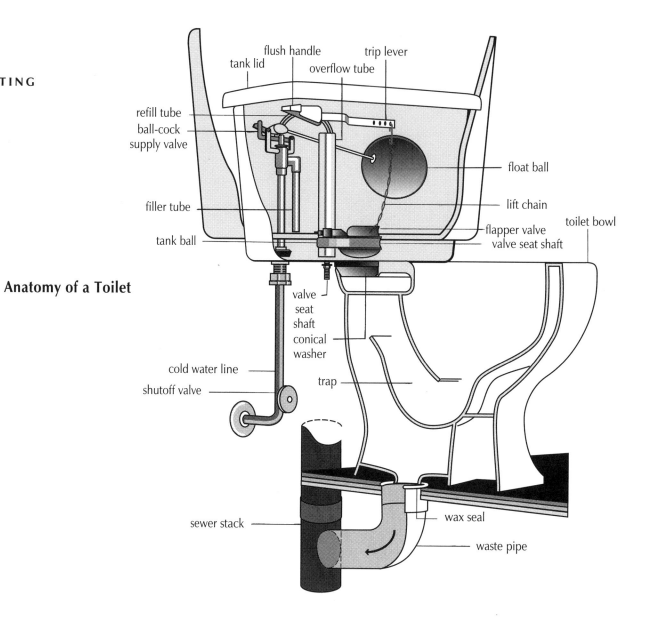

tank lid

flush handle

trip lever

overflow tube

refill tube

ball-cock
supply valve

float ball

filler tube

lift chain

tank ball

flapper valve
valve seat shaft

toilet bowl

Anatomy of a Toilet

valve
seat
shaft
conical
washer

cold water line

trap

shutoff valve

sewer stack

wax seal

waste pipe

PLUMB OUT OF
YOUR MIND

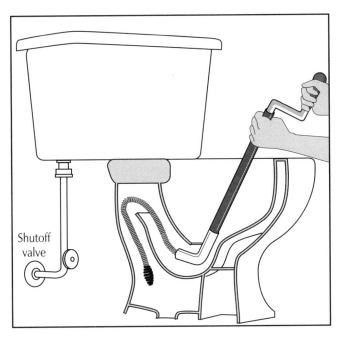

Using a Closet Auger

Problem

A ghost is flushing the toilet.

Possible Causes

The flush valve seat is dirty.
The lift chain needs adjusting.
The float ball is faulty or float rod is bent.

Solution

Close the water shutoff valve and flush the toilet. Dry up the remaining water in the tank. Clean off the valve seat with paper towels or a sponge.

With a flapper valve, unhook its chain from the trip lever, noting into which hole the chain is hooked. Some flapper valves fit over the overflow tube; slide it off. If attached to hooks on the side of the overflow tube, unhook. Install the new valve.

Sewer Lines and the Main Drain

Unclogging these lines means dealing with raw sewage. It can be messy. Try flushing the sewer line with a garden hose but don't let the water run more than a minute. It could back up and cause an overflow. If flushing has no effect, you may need to rent an auger used for drains and sewers versus the kind used for fixture traps. Clearing the drain will require a longer, stronger, motorized auger. It also might be a two-person operation. But if you are game here's what to do. You will need to access the cleanout, which is a Y-shaped fitting mounted on the drain generally near the bottom of the home's soil stack. Open the cleanout plug and insert the spiral cutting end of the auger into the drain. It is the rare clog that does not respond to the power of the auger.

However, sometimes tree roots invade the drain pipes and cause stoppages. It would be more economical and practical to hire a professional drain-clearing service to remove roots, which can be stubborn. Doing the job your inexperienced self could cost you far more in equipment and tool rental and time.

The Big Bang

All plumbing is subject to a variety of distracting noises. One of the most irritating is water hammer—that loud bang that occurs from a sudden stop in the flow of fresh water when you turn off a fast-closing faucet, or when the washing machine or dishwasher shuts off. Until now you may have resigned yourself to living with it but you don't have to.

How many times have you asked what causes the big bang and have been told it is air in the line? You've even repeated it as part of your apology to visitors who are startled out of their designer underwear when it happens. But guess what? It's not entirely true. The answer depends on whether you are talking about fresh-water supply pipes or heating pipes.

Air in the line will cause noises in steam and hot water heating systems. But when the big bang occurs in the fresh-water pipes it is because of the *absence* of air in the line. Air plays a special role in the pipes, providing a cushion for rushing water.

Air generally is provided to these fresh-water pipe lines by air chambers. The chambers take the strain off the pipes by providing a cushion of air for rushing water to bounce against when a valve closes. The air chambers are extensions attached to the water pipes and located not far from a shutoff valve.

You may have seen a short pipe the same diameter as the supply pipe or a little larger with a cap on the end. It saddles the supply pipe and rises up in the air in a dead end. The cap traps air inside the twelve-inch-long chamber. In some homes the air chamber may be located behind a wall and therefore not visible. But if there are any air chambers at all on your system you should see at least one somewhere, since they would or should be located on every hot and cold water pipe leading to a fixture. For example, there should be one at the furnace, the hot water heater, the dishwasher, a sink, and so on. A plumbing system with improperly operating air chambers, or one that does not have them, would experience the bang.

Air can be introduced or restored to the line in one of three ways: draining the system, installing air chambers, or installing water shock arrestors.

To **drain the system** start by turning off the water supply at the main shutoff valve or switch off the submersible pump. Turn off the power to the hot water heater and the furnace. If the water heater is gas-fired, turn off the main gas valve. Go through the house and open every faucet, including outside ones, and flush every toilet. Bale and sponge out all remaining water in the toilets. Drain the furnace and the water heater by opening their faucets. If you have a private water system, drain the holding tank and any water treatment equipment. If you have a hot-water heating system, open the valves on all of the radiators in the house and unscrew an air vent from a radiator on the top floor. This will maintain air pressure as the heating lines drain into the furnace.

Then, go back to the basement and open the **drain faucet** on the main supply. Hopefully, you have one. Not all houses do. If you don't, you still can do the job, but you might want to have one installed for convenience.

Next, turn the water back on and dash through the house like a madwoman shutting off the faucets. That should be fun.

Do not turn the water back on if you plan to be away from the house for the winter season or during very cold weather. Water that remains in the pipes during cold weather can freeze and burst pipes and crack traps and toilet bowls. For shorter absences, opening a spigot to a slow drizzle relieves the pressure in the line by keeping the water moving. Moving water does not freeze. However, this is wasteful and not cost-effective.

Instead, pour antifreeze into all of the sinks, tubs, showers, washing machine takeout pipe, and toilet bowls so that the traps will have the liquid necessary to block waste gases and the danger of freezing will be minimized.

Some pipe noises are caused by the vibration of rushing water knocking pipes against the subflooring and floor joists. You may want to check to see if one or more pipes have a loose or missing hanger strap or not enough support. Installing a pipe strap or hanger and rubber pipe insulation where the pipe crosses a joist would cushion the blow.

Shock arrestors are a bit more costly than air chambers but serve the same purpose. Over time, the water level in an air chamber slowly rises and absorbs the air trapped in the chamber. When most of the air is gone, water hammer or banging in the pipes occurs. Shock arrestors absorb hydraulic shock when a faucet or valve is closed quickly.

Air Chamber Position on Fresh Water Supply Pipe

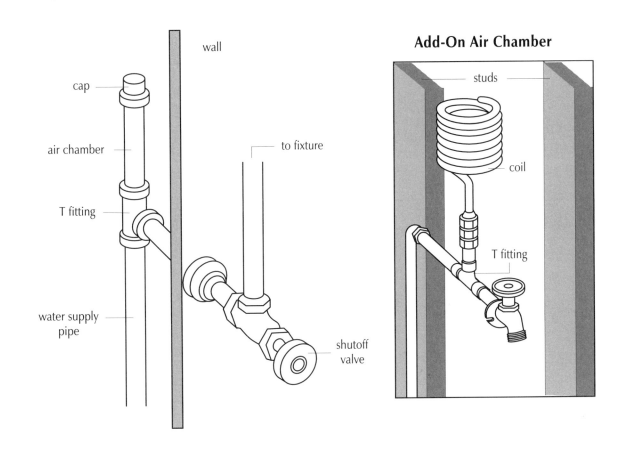

Add-On Air Chamber

Preventing—and When It Is Too Late, Thawing—Frozen Pipes

If your tap delivers nice, icy cold water during the dead of winter, your pipes may be trying to tell you something: They are too cold. They are prime candidates for freezing. Especially vulnerable are water pipes that run up through the exterior walls of the house. A home's heating system does not protect them. If any of your water pipes are located behind an outside wall you may want to consider having the walls professionally packed with insulation that is blown between the outside and inside walls with special equipment. For those pipes inside, insulate them with pre-split foam tubing or pipe jackets. Electric heat tape is a great pipe protector. The thermostatically controlled device is wrapped around the pipe with one end plugged into an electrical outlet. It uses only a small amount of current, but the drawback is it won't work when there is a power outage, which is exactly when your house will require protection against freezing temperatures. (As an emergency preventive until you get the pipes insulated, let water trickle through the line of a faucet at the lowest part of the house, usually the basement.)

Make a habit just as the weather turns cold to turn off the water supply to outside spigots and drain those pipes. Wrap the pipes with insulation as an extra precaution should some water remain in the line after draining.

Yikes! The pipes are frozen. You can tell because water drizzles out or not at all when you turn on the faucet. You can defrost the pipes safely in a couple of ways. As a precaution, **always** start defrosting at the faucet end of the line. Defrosting produces steam and unmelted ice could block the line preventing the resulting steam from escaping. A buildup of pressure could burst the pipe.

You can defrost the pipes by wrapping them with electric heating tape or warming them with a heat lamp, a hair dryer, or a flame spreader affixed to a butane torch. If using any of the latter three, do not train the heat on one part of the pipe for long stretches. Keep the device moving along the pipe so that you don't get any part of the pipe hot enough to burn you if touched. Be especially attentive when using the open flame of a butane torch.

5

YOU GIVE ME FEVER: HEATING AND COOLING SYSTEMS

Monster in the Basement

When I was a little girl my father assigned each of us kids weekly chores. My two older brothers polished the brass fixtures on the outside doors and washed the windows. My sister mopped the floors, dusted, and helped my mother prepare meals. My single job was: the furnace. I dreaded it. The furnace was a monster in my child view. Sometimes I'd pay off one of my brothers to do my job. But when I ran out of bribe money, I had to do the task myself.

The job entailed checking the water level in the furnace twice a week. When my father assigned me the duty, he gravely warned me that letting the furnace "go dry" could mean an explosion and possible fire. Years later, I wondered why such an important assignment, with death and destruction a certain consequence of negligence, was entrusted to an eight-year-old—a known scaredy-cat of an eight-year-old at that. I have since concluded that my father believed that his girl child needed a challenging chore that would earn her the respect of expertise that society gives its males just for being their male selves and for which she and her sister females would have to prove themselves repeatedly, expertise notwithstanding.

However, it was a bit too much of a challenge. My fears were fueled not only by the dark, dank cellar but by a collection of children's books that sat just outside the furnace room in a bookcase. One of the books was a Rudyard Kipling tale with a color illustration of a tiger with its fangs and claws bared. It haunted me. Each time I finished my furnace gig, I'd have nightmares of the beast chasing and nearly catching me.

With that image in my head, I crept into the cellar on unsteady legs, a flashlight in one hand and a broom in the other to ward off whatever dangers in the dark might jump out at me. On the assigned furnace day, I checked the water level by looking into the slim glass water gauge mounted on the outside of the furnace. It was always clogged with rust, which made the water line difficult to see. To make matters worse, fear made my eyes play tricks on me. Once, my eyes told me that the furnace did not need water, so I ran out without filling it. A day later, the furnace "went dry" and exploded.

Decades later the memory of that incident kept me frozen in my tracks the day the heat would not come on and I had to confront the furnace to find out why. Unlike the ill-fated oil burner of my youth, this one was fueled by gas. It had an automatic water feeder and low-water cutoff, which made it less likely that it would "go dry." Still, memories of the exploding furnace of my childhood sapped my courage.

Water was visible in the glass, indicating that it did not need to be filled. Yet, it was not working. I didn't know what else to look for and was timid about exploration. Discouraged, I went back upstairs to the kitchen, wishing I wasn't such a coward. Calling a heating company would have been the obvious thing to do, but I didn't have enough money to even fake a payment with a postdated check.

YOU GIVE ME FEVER:
HEATING AND
COOLING SYSTEMS

I decided to eat an omelette. Sound familiar? I turned on the gas stove and got the familiar hissing sound but no flames. Without hesitation I opened the range top and relit the pilot. Suddenly an epiphany. That was it. The pilot probably had blown out on the furnace. I remembered that is what happened the previous year and my neighbor handled it. Unfortunately I didn't ask any questions then and now no one was around and I was uncertain what to do.

Where was the pilot? I returned to the basement and checked the diagram taped to the burner and traced the location of the pilot at the bottom of the furnace. I got down on my knees and looked in. There was no flame. I grabbed a box of long fireplace matches, lit one, and touched it to the pilot. I tried it a few times. Each time, the pilot lit up but the flame would not hold. I knew that occasionally the pilot light on a furnace blows out. However, I did not know that, unlike stoves, the furnace has a safety feature that automatically shuts down the gas line to prevent gas from escaping into the air. A gas escape would be disastrous considering that typical of most homes my furnace was seated next to the hot water heater, which has an open flame.

I leafed through my homeowners repair books and read that I would have to turn the pilot button to On, push it in, and hold it in while I lit the pilot. I tried that. It didn't work.

I swallowed my pride and called an old friend to borrow the money to pay for a visit from a heating company. "Did you hold the button in for forty-five seconds after you lit the pilot?" he asked. The question seemed insignificant at first. Sure I held the button in but no I hadn't paid attention for how long. He suggested that I try that first.

I went back to the basement to try again. I struck a match, touched the flame to the pilot, and held the pilot button in for a full forty-five-second count. That was it. The flame held, the furnace roared. Steam hissed from the radiators. The house was warm again, and finally I had made peace with the monster in the basement.

Of course, I wondered why none of the three homeowners manuals I consulted made no mention of the critical detail of holding in the pilot button for a full forty-five seconds. Nonetheless, at some point you will have to come face-to-face with your furnace, and it does not have to be as traumatic as the encounters I have had. Introduce yourself to your furnace and get to know it before there is a crisis.

Relighting the Pilot on a Gas Burner

Not All Are Alike

There are several home heating systems, and even if you have one identical to your next door neighbor's, your house is not going to have the same heating experience, neither comfortwise nor costwise. Unique conditions in your home dictate what level and consistency of comfort your heating system provides. Where the house is located, the number of rooms and their sizes, the landscaping, the number of family members, the amount of furniture in the house, and the frequency of use of such large heat-producing appliances as the stove and oven as well as where they are situated are all controlling factors. Even with those factors taken into consideration, no heating system heats all rooms in the house to the same degree. The farther the room is from the heat source the cooler it is likely to be. Unfortunately, that's normal.

Identifying Your Heating System

Most homes are warmed by a central heating system as opposed to a direct heat system, like what is provided by a fireplace or wood stove. The central system typically comprises three distinct components: the heat source, the heat exchanger, and the heat distributor.

Heat Source

Heat is generated by wood, oil, gas, the sun, a heat pump, or an electric baseboard heater.

Heat Exchanger

The heat source is connected to the heat exchanger unit. The unit often is referred to in generic terms as the furnace. However, it is a furnace only if it heats air. It's a boiler if it heats water for a hot water or radiant heat system, or creates steam for a steam heat system.

Heat Distributor

Pipes, radiators, blowers, and vents distribute the warmth provided by the energy source and exchanger. In a **steam heat system,** the boiler heats up water and creates steam, which rises under its own pressure through pipes and into radiators that are located in individual rooms in the house. As the steam cools down, it condenses back to water and returns to the boiler to be heated again and resume the cycle.

The water in a **hot water system** reaches the radiators in one of two ways—either by a circulator pump or by gravity. Because hot water is lighter than cold water, it rises through the pipes and the radiators. When it cools, it drops down and returns to the boiler to be heated again.

In a **hot-air system,** a fan pulls the air into the heat exchanger and blows it through ducts to hot air registers warming the room, and resuming the cycle.

Radiant heat requires no ductwork and no visible radiators or pipes. This kind of heating system is found in some old homes and in public buildings. Like the steam and hot water heating system, the heat in this system is generated by a boiler that heats water, which is conveyed through pipes located under the flooring and/or behind walls or ceilings.

Forced Hot Water Heating System

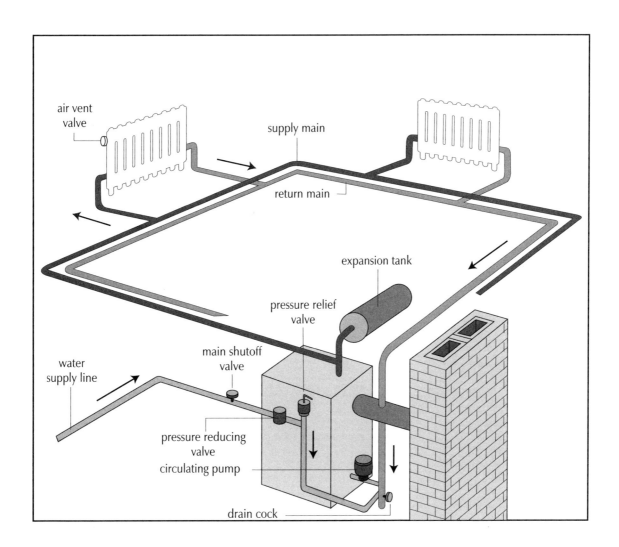

air vent
valve

supply main

return main

expansion tank

pressure relief
valve

main shutoff
valve

water
supply line

pressure reducing
valve

circulating pump

drain cock

Times Have Changed

Fifty years ago, coal was the fuel of choice for home heating. But eventually coal gave way to cleaner-burning oil, which began losing ground to even cleaner-burning gas during the oil embargo years of the 1970s. These days, the electric heat pump is growing in popularity in new construction and may one day even become popular with homeowners if the techies ever work out the bugs. It is regarded as the most efficient. Solar heating systems are scattered throughout the country, although they have not caught on as a widely used system. Although this is an efficient, nature-friendly system, it still has an experimental personality.

Is It Hot Water or Steam?

A hot water and steam radiator system look almost alike. However, you can tell them apart easily by looking at the radiators. On one side of a steam radiator there is an air vent that looks like a miniature silo with a little numbered dial on its head. The vent's purpose is to control the steam pressure. No such valve is present on radiators in a hot water system.

STEAM HEATING SYSTEMS

My old steam heating system was typically noisy with radiators and pipes that hissed and banged. They are unnerving sounds that were most noticeable when visitors came by. I had no clue I would ever miss them. But when I moved into a place with a heat pump system, I found I had a longing for the cozy hiss and bang that had come to mean home on cold winter nights. Of course, the fans on the heat pumps have their own

**YOU GIVE ME FEVER:
HEATING AND
COOLING SYSTEMS**

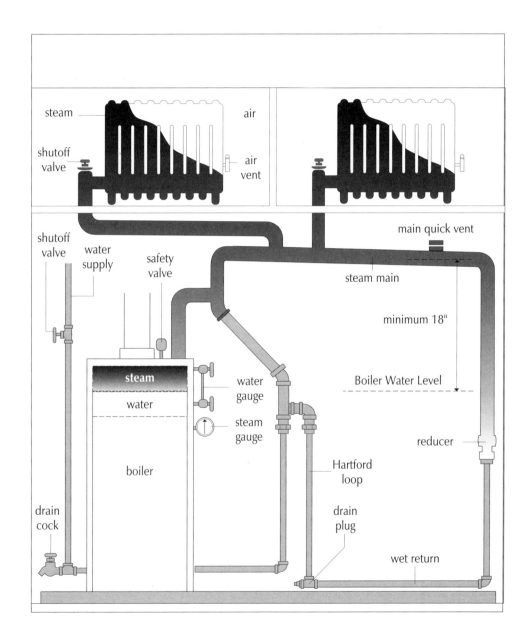

steam

air

shutoff
valve

air
vent

shutoff
valve

water
supply

safety
valve

main quick vent

steam main

minimum 18"

Boiler Water Level

water
gauge

steam

water

steam
gauge

boiler

reducer

Hartford
loop

drain
cock

drain
plug

wet return

Steam Heating System

sounds but nothing quite as comforting as what I became accustomed to in steam heating systems.

Found chiefly in older homes, the steam system has not survived into new construction. It is an intimidating-looking arrangement of pipes and gauges but is a pussycat to manage when you know what to do.

MAINTENANCE

Get a service contract through your local utility company. It's cheap insurance if something major breaks down on the furnace or hot water heater.

Flush the boiler at least once a month, during the heating season.

To flush the boiler:

1. Open the air vents on the radiators located on the highest level of the house.

2. Turn off boiler's power switch.

3. Shut off the boiler's water supply.

4. Attach one end of a garden hose to the drain cock (faucet) at the lowest part of the boiler (usually at the rear of the boiler) and lead the other end of the hose into a drain or bucket.

5. Open the faucet and let the line drain through the hose. The water most likely will be heavy and brown with rust and sediment.

6. When that flow slows, turn the water supply back on and flush the boiler with fresh water.

7. When the water from the boiler runs clear, turn off the drain cock (faucet).

8. Refill the boiler by opening the water supply until the boiler reaches

its proper water level. The glass water-level indicator should be slightly more than half full.

9. Turn the boiler back on.

10. When you can hear water filling the pipes, return to the top-floor radiators and close the air vents.

11. Open and close the vents on all the other radiators in the house to let whatever air trapped within escape.

BLEEDING RADIATORS

Water in the radiator or the radiator's air vent in a steam system prevents the radiator from heating. To fix the problem, you have to bleed the radiators. To do so, unscrew the air vent and shake any water out. Using a pipe wrench, disconnect the radiator by unscrewing the connection to the steam pipe. Tilt the radiator on its side to drain any water that may be trapped within into a pan. The radiator is heavy cast iron. You will need a helping hand to do this.

Troubleshooting a Steam System

Problem	Possible Cause	Solution
No heat	Pilot out on burner.	Relight pilot.
	Low water level in boiler.	Fill boiler until gauge glass is half full.
	Blown fuse or tripped circuit breaker.	Replace fuse or reset breaker.

Problem	Possible Cause	Solution
Cold radiator	Closed radiator valve.	Fully open valve.
	Water in air vent and or radiator.	Unscrew air vent and shake any water out of it. Uncouple radiator from pipe fitting and turn it on end and drain. (You will need help lifting it.)
	Radiator sitting flat.	Place level on top of radiator to determine if it is sitting flat. If it is, gradually tilt radiator toward the end with the steam shutoff valve and insert small pieces of wood under the radiator feet on the opposite end. Take care not to tilt too far or connection to radiator's supply pipe could be damaged. (You will need help lifting the radiator.)
Air vent spitting water	Water in vent.	Unscrew vent, shake out water.
Banging radiator	Water trapped in radiator.	Tilt radiator toward shutoff valve and insert shims under radiator feet.

Hot-Water Heating System: Maintenance

Periodically flush boiler and bleed radiators as instructed above. Invest in an automatic valve for radiators to eliminate the need for bleeding or venting the radiators by hand. But if you must do it by hand, while the system is on, open the vent knob on the radiator and release the air until water begins to spurt through. Close the vent knob.

Troubleshooting an Electric Heat Pump

Heat pumps work best in regions with mild winters and hot, humid summers. The heat pump concept is remarkable. In winter, it draws heat from outside air and pumps it indoors through vents. Even thirty-degree temperatures have heat the pump can tap. However, efficiency plummets significantly when the temperature outside takes a substantial dive. The condenser coils frost over, blocking them from their heat source. When this happens, a supplementary heater kicks in to supply indoor warmth. You'll notice how dramatically more costly this supplementary heat is when the utility bill arrives.

In the summer season the pump reverses itself for cooling and transfers the warmth in the indoor air to the outside.

During extremely cold temperatures, the pump's outdoor coils could frost over. The equipment is designed to defrost itself by switching over to the cooling mode to draw the warm indoor air over the coils to melt the frost. However, if that does not happen, you may have to help it along by manually shifting the controls between heating and cooling at up to fifteen-minute intervals for about an hour. If that does not work you'll have to make that fateful call to the heat pump doctor.

106

RENOVATING
WOMAN

Troubleshooting a Gas Burner

1. Check for blown fuse or tripped circuit breaker.

2. Read directions on the furnace for lighting the pilot.

3. If pilot is out, relight. If flame won't catch, check for dirt that may be clogging the pilot's tiny opening. Clean the opening by poking it with a thin copper wire.

4. If pilot flame won't hold, be certain you've held in the pilot button for at least forty-five seconds after the flame catches.

5. If pilot light will not stay lit, the flame may be too high or too short to make proper contact with the thermocoupler. Gradually turn the pilot screw to adjust the flame to extend out and upward.

Troubleshooting an Oil Burner

1. Check for a blown fuse or tripped circuit breaker.

2. Move the thermostat control up a few degrees to see if the furnace kicks on.

3. Make sure the master switch is on. There may be two of these, one at the burner and one in a convenient location away from the burner, perhaps at the top of the basement steps.

4. Check the gauge to be sure the tank is not out of oil. If there is no gauge, use a dipstick the way you would check for oil in the car. The gauge could be broken, so even if there is one, double-check by the dipstick method.

5. Press the ignition safety control's reset button on the burner and the restart button on the motor.

Energy-Saving Heating Tips

- For each degree you lower your thermostat below seventy-three degrees F you will save about 4 percent on heating costs.
- During the winter, for systems other than heat pumps, set your thermostat at seventy degrees F or lower during the day and sixty-five degrees F at night.
- If you have a heat pump, do not set it back at night unless you have a programmable thermostat specifically designed for heat pumps. Raising the thermostat manually on a heat pump after a nighttime setback in winter causes the auxiliary heat to come on. This backup heat diminishes any savings gained during the setback period. A programmable thermostat allows the heat pump greater recovery time so that it gradually recovers the temperature with very little or no expensive auxiliary heat.
- Turn off heat source in seldom used or unused rooms.
- Insulate the attic.
- Keep the furnace and ductwork dust free and check the furnace filter monthly. Clean or change the filter as necessary.

Energy-Saving Cooling Tips

- Make frequent maintenance checks and repair any mechanical problems **promptly.**
- If you have a central air conditioner, set the thermostat at seventy-

eight degrees F or higher. For every degree you raise your thermostat setting above seventy-two F you will save about 7 percent on cooling costs, according to the experts.

- Install a programmable thermostat for better control of the cooling and heating system. It can save you on average up to 25 percent on your cooling and heating costs.
- Change filters in both window units and central air-conditioning units at least once a month.
- Be certain that drapes, furniture, and carpets don't block vents.
- Shade your air conditioner with shrubs or an awning to keep the system from working too hard. Always keep the outdoor unit clear of obstructions.
- If you have an attic but cannot afford a whole-house or attic fan, use window fans with a feature that draws air out of a room. Since hot air rises, the fan will pull the heat rising from the lower floors and send it out the window.

Cleaning an External Central Air Unit

- Turn the power off at the service panel, that is, the circuit breaker or fuse box.
- Unscrew the condenser unit cover. Then unscrew the fan. On some units you won't have to unscrew the fan since it will come out when the cover is lifted.
- Cover the electrical parts with plastic sheeting and secure it with duct tape. Use your hand to sweep out leaves and other loose debris.
- With a soft brush, gently brush the dirt from the condenser coils.
- Next, clean the fan blades with a soft brush and noncaustic deter-

gent. Using a garden hose, spray the fan blades, the coils, and inside the unit with water until the wash water runs clear.

- Check at your local hardware or home improvement store for filters that screen out pollen, leaves and other debris.
- If your home is dry in the winter, have a humidifier installed. Moist air is warmer than dry air and it will help you feel more comfortable at lower temperatures.

It's Cold in Here! It's Hot in Here!

Some people complain that they are just throwing money out the window when it comes to adequately heating their living space. The air inside is cold in the winter and the air-conditioning can't get you cool enough in the summer months. Well, poorly insulated windows are the obvious routes for the great escape of your cash. But you would be surprised where else your money makes a quick getaway.

It could be drawn through places that do not need conditioned air such as behind wall receptacles and light switches, and not just the ones on the outside walls. It leaves through ceiling light fixtures—particularly recessed lighting, under and around doors, and through the seams of window frames.

You can pinpoint the escape routes yourself or with the help of your local utility company, which should offer a home energy efficiency evaluation as a service. I had my utility company, BGE, evaluate the efficiency of my living space. I admit that at the time I was a skeptic trying to satisfy my curiosity. After all, the more money I spend trying to heat and cool my space the more money the utility company makes; isn't that the idea? To a point yes. But our natural resources in fossil fuels and electricity are dwindling. Utility companies realize, or should, that you can't survive economically if you have nothing to sell. Just as a matter of course, conservation should be a conscious part of how we live our lives whether there is money to be saved or not.

We made some surprising discoveries with my home evaluation. For one, central heating and cooling systems are only as effective as the insulation in the home they are serving. These systems rely on good air circulation and good sealing of areas that do not need conditioned air, such as crawl spaces and behind electrical outlets.

I was losing an enormous amount of energy into the recessed lighting and behind the wall switches and receptacles in my home. My heat pump works by recycling air but it had to work extra hard because I had something blocking the return air vent. The utility did an elaborate test with fancy equipment outfitted with impressive dials and color tubes to determine the level of air changes in my living space. You want to have good insulation and sealing but you don't want static or stale air. The evaluator pinpointed the most egregious air escape routes. But anyone can do their own evaluation with a tool as simple as a plastic container of baby powder with the little sifting holes on top.

THE TEST

► **REAL MAN
TIP:**

A real man will let you
show him how to flush the
furnace if he doesn't
already know.

Choose a breezy day in any season. Close all of the windows and doors. Then, go to each window, door, fireplace, electrical outlet, and recessed light fixture and squirt powder near it. Watch where the powder goes. If it merely hangs in the air before drifting downward, then you have an excellently insulated whatever. Otherwise, you will see the powder being pulled or directed to where the air and your money are going—out the window, up the chimney, and so on.

You can block these escape routes yourself inexpensively. Caulk around the windows either outside or inside, depending on accessibility and/or your aesthetics. Caulking is available in a few colors, including black, white, almond, and clear. Draft stopper insulation pads customized for switch outlets and receptacles are available in packages of a dozen and cost about eighty-eight cents for the package. Check the damper on the chimney.

Seal seams on furnace heat stacks. A good product to use for this is stringless foil tape. It is a higher performer than the typical gray duct tape, which breaks down after a few years and is not truly heat- and cold-resistant. Insulate the screw hole openings in the housing of recessed lighting. Insulate around outside doorjambs with felt weather stripping, whether you live in a detached house or a high-rise condominium. (Tall buildings are famous for drafts.)

6

UP ON THE ROOF

When considering a house purchase, home buyers will ask the sellers exhaustive questions about the roof and even demand a warranty that it will remain sound for the next twenty years. But it is the rare buyer who will personally inspect the roof from up top. Once the furniture has been moved in, many homeowners give little if any thought to the roof unless, of course, it has a leak. The reason for this avoidance is understandable. Fear! After all, the roof is way up there!

Nonetheless, roof inspection should be a routine item on every homeowner's annual home maintenance checklist, and you don't have to drag the ladder out each time to do it. At the very least use a strong pair of binoculars to check out the sides, front and back. If you can battle past your fears, go on up and look, even if you do it just one time. Your perspective will be so much more informed if you ever have to hire a roofer for serious roof work.

Signs of Trouble

If you find pieces of slate or asphalt tiling around the periphery of the house, the roofing material needs to be inspected for breakage and bare spots. Tiles with curled edges are not doing their job; water probably is getting underneath. A large accumulation of granules in the gutters is a sign that the roof's coating is deteriorating. Crumbled asphalt in the gutters is a sign that the asphalt shingles are breaking down. The solution may range from replacing individual tiles to redoing a section, or re-roofing altogether.

The **roof** is a home's first line of defense against the substantial elements of wind, rain, snow, hail, and the damaging rays of the sun. It is designed with a pitch to shed rain and snow. A roof's material and construction should be able to provide weatherproofing that can hold up for at least thirty years in areas that don't experience long seasons of the severest bouts of heat, cold, or precipitation.

ROOF DESIGNS

Next to fire, water is one natural element that can cause serious damage. Most residential roofs are **pitched** or **sloped** to allow water to run off into gutters and downspouts and away from the house. Some homes are built with **flat** or low-sloping roofs, but even those are designed with enough of a pitch to permit water drainage.

TYPES OF ROOFING MATERIALS

Asphalt shingle or tiles, slate tiles, clay tiles, and wood shakes are most commonly used on pitched roofs. There are a few places that use corrugated steel or aluminum. Asphalt shingles are a composition of fiberglass and asphalt. You might also hear about organic composition shingles, which are made up of wood and paper fibers. **Slate tiles** are a combination of shale and clay. They are a bear to work with when they have aged. Few houses are constructed these days with slate roofs. Over time, the material becomes brittle and difficult to repair because slate tiles can crack under the pressure of walking on them while attempting to reach the damaged area. Companies that manufacture slate tiles are becoming rare as well. And even roofing companies that advertise themselves as "slate roof experts" start off by trying to convince you to redo the entire roof with asphalt shingle. Their idea of repairing the roof is replacing it with something else.

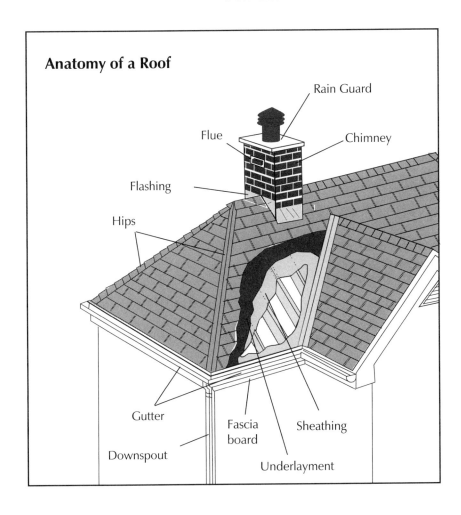

Anatomy of a Roof

Rain Guard

Flue

Chimney

Flashing

Hips

Gutter

Fascia board

Sheathing

Downspout

Underlayment

LAYERS FROM THE INSIDE OUT: PITCHED ROOFS

1. **Rafters** made of two-by-fours provide the form and frame for the roof.

2. The **deck** or **subroof,** which consists of plywood or fiberboard **sheathing,** is nailed to the rafters as a base for the top layers of roofing material.

3. **Underlayment** is roofing paper, which is rolled out over the plywood sheathing. It is the second line of waterproofing. It is thin enough to allow house moisture to escape through it and thick enough to prevent rain penetration. It is a heavy, black, fibrous paper that has been treated with asphalt.

4. **Asphalt shingles, slate, or tile** form the last layer and are the first line of protection from the weather. The shingles come in four-foot lengths and are overlapped and nailed down for the most effective weatherproofing.

5. **Flashing material,** made of copper, aluminum, or some other thin metal sheeting, is applied around the chimney, vent pipes, and skylights—anywhere there is an interruption of roofing tile. Flashing also is installed along the roof's hips and valleys (the joints) to prevent water seepage.

6. Sometimes, a bead of **roofing cement** is applied with a caulking gun along the seams where the roof meets the house facade, such as with a porch roof.

FLAT ROOFS

Flat roofs generally are referred to as **built-up** roofs. Their lifespan of up to twenty years is shorter than that of the sloped roof. A flat roof is built or should be built with a slight pitch to allow for runoff. The roof comprises several alternating layers of **roofing paper** and **roofing tar** or **asphalt.** The tar is mopped on either hot or cold. The final surface is an application of **crushed gravel.**

Leaks

Finding leaks on a pitched roof takes a very patient detective. **Do not** attempt to go on the roof in bad weather. With a pitched roof, it is probable that the site where the water is showing up is not the origin of the leak. More than likely, the damp spot is merely the end of the leak path. The source of the problem is higher up. By process of elimination, if the leak is showing up in the ceiling on the same side of the house as the chimney, for example, start by checking the integrity of the flashing around the chimney. Is the flashing loose or missing? Are the roofing tiles in the general vicinity of the chimney intact?

If you have an unfinished attic, the leak can be detected more easily from the underside of the roof while it is raining. Use a strong flashlight to find wet spots. You will have to remove any insulation batting that is between the rafters. **(Note: Since the insulation is made of fiberglass you will want to wear gloves and a long-sleeved shirt to protect your skin and goggles to keep the fibers from getting in your eyes.)**

After you have located the leak from the inside, clearly mark the spot so you can easily find it later. When the rain stops, drive a long nail or wire through the marked spot so that the nail can be seen topside and you can find the exact point of the leak. The repair solution might call for an application of roofing cement on the site of the damage and/or replacing a section of tile.

If the attic ceiling is finished, finding the leak is a bit more tricky. You can get a general idea of where the hole is by measuring back from the wet spot to the likely high point. It will be a guessing game. But once you are on the roof, the source may be easily evident as cracked or missing pieces of roofing tile or loose flashing. If any area of the roof is soft or gives with pressure, there are structural problems such as wood rot that will require more extensive attention. Carpentry skills and special tools will be required so you may have to call in a professional roofer.

FLAT ROOFS

Homes with flat roofs usually have a built-up roof or rolled roof. A leak on a built-up or rolled roof is easy to find since, unlike a steeply pitched roof, it is more accessible for climbing. Also the source of the leak will be directly above the wet spot of the ceiling. Built-up or rolled roofs are designed slightly pitched so that water will drain into a gutter or downspout. But sometimes there are low spots where water pools, and over time a leak will develop in the weakened area. Built-up and rolled roofs also tend to experience blisters in the asphalt where the gravel has blown away. When the blisters split, a source of leakage opens up.

To repair a blister on a built-up or rolled roof:

1. Sweep the gravel aside with a stiff bristled brush.

2. Slash the blister open with a utility knife. Use a putty knife to work roofing cement under the edges and on top of and around the slash.

3. Create a patch made of asphalt tile or roofing paper that will completely fit over the repair area. Nail the patch down and cover it with a generous coating of roofing cement.

Gutters and Leaders (Downspouts)

Every time we got a good rainfall, the basement of my house took on water. We, the urban homeowner couple, responded by slathering waterproof wash on the stone foundation walls, pumping silicone caulking into the cracks, and otherwise doing every desperate thing we learned from sidewalk quarterbacks but the right thing. The Ex and I treated the symptoms rather than the cause. It wasn't until it was just me and the house left to get along with each other that I discovered the cause.

It happened one warm, rainy day whilst I was sitting out on the back porch counting raindrops and otherwise contemplating my life during a short but intense deluge. After a while, the runoff from one side of the house sounded like a small Niagara. I looked over the porch rail and noticed that water was cascading over the edge of the gutter, forming a pool against the foundation of the house. It was the side of the house where the basement took on water.

I'm smart, so I said to myself: "Self, something's stopping up the gutter and downspout." When the rain stopped, I called a handyman I knew who had a very tall ladder, and since this was back in my "trust-in-my-fellowman" days, I paid him to go up and investigate the problem.

He found a pet cemetery and compost pile. From the gutter he pulled out a mass of leaves, twigs, and sprouting vegetation. There was a squirrel that had lost its little way and died wedged in the downspout. One section of gutter was so off pitch that instead of draining water away it was providing a ten-foot birdbath for the neighborhood crows. So it did not come as a surprise to him that there were birds' nests there, one with a nearly born bird still partially in its shell and not far along the way a rather large pigeon, both dead.

The problem with the wet basement was the gutters. More accurately, the problem with the wet basement was that in a dozen years its big-time, university-educated homeowners never made a routine of cleaning out the gutters on even an annual basis. It never crossed our minds that it was important to do that more than the one time we installed mesh leaf strainers on the lower-level porch roof. The upper roof got no attention. We didn't even own a tall ladder and didn't try to make friends with anyone who did. So from season to season the gutter trays became a repository for everything that ever landed on it. In fact, I don't recall seeing anyone in the neighborhood cleaning their gutters. They obviously were university grads too.

Once my gutters and downspouts were dredged, flushed, sealed at the seams, and the runoff directed away from the house, the basement ceased to get wet from a rainfall. Oftentimes, simple solutions await those of us who use our brains. I had made no serious connection between the purpose of downspouts and gutters and a wet basement. I thought the gutters were there so that water from the roof would not drip down my back when I entered the house. Surprisingly, a lot of allegedly intelligent homeowners don't appear to get the connection between the work the gutters do and the continued soundness of the house.

Of course, the necessity for gutters and downspouts is considerable. To ignore them is to court trouble. When debris is allowed to accumulate in these water transport systems as mine did, rainwater has nowhere to go but over the side. The overhang to which the gutters are attached and the fascia boards located beneath get soaked, then dry out and soaked again. Over time if this activity continues unchecked, these roof parts will rot away.

Inspect your downspouts and gutters. Make certain that the gutters are pitched at an angle that allows the water to flow away. Check that downspouts are turned away from the house. Rest their terminal end on a plastic or concrete **splashblock** angled on a downward slope away from the foundation of the house.

Another water diverter is a rolled plastic sleeve, which is attached to the end of the downspout. When water fills the sleeve, it unfurls, channeling the water away from the house.

A **dry well** is the best method of keeping water away from a home's foundation. It is especially useful in wet climates and where there is no

A Dry Well System

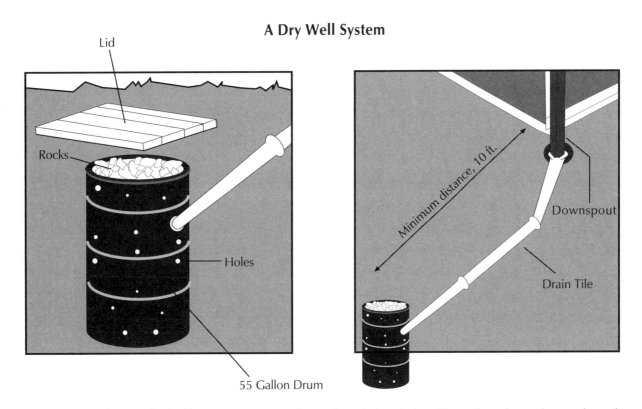

A dry well is the best method of keeping water away from a home's foundation. The well can be made out of an oil drum, concrete blocks and stones. It is set a minimum of eighteen inches below ground ten feet away from the house. The home's downspout is connected to drainage tiles that are set into the side of the oil drum. Punctures in the body of the drum allow water to seep slowly into the soil and a lid keeps dirt from settling into the well.

storm drain nearby. The well is set at least eighteen inches underground and ten feet away from the house foundation. The downspout is connected to drainage tiles that lead directly into the side of the oil drum.

An inexpensive, effective well can be made out of a fifty-five-gallon oil drum. Cut off each end of the drum. Make random punctures in the body of the drum. These little openings will allow any captured water to slowly drain into the underground. **(See Chapter 13 for the dangers of residential runoff.)** Using a hole saw, cut a hole in the side of the drum nearest the top large enough to insert the drainage tile (pipe). Set the drum in the ground and fill it with rocks or broken concrete. Insert the drainage tile in the hole that was cut into the side of the drum. Connect the downspout to the end of the drainage tile near the house. Cover the top of the drum with something solid, like wood, sheet metal, or a block of concrete to keep soil from settling into it. Refill the cavity with dirt.

MAINTAINING GUTTERS AND DOWNSPOUTS

Roof gutters should be cleaned at least twice a year—during the waning days of autumn and again toward the end of spring except if you live in the woods, whereupon more frequent attention should be given. During autumn and spring nature dispenses the leaves and seeds that can clog gutters and spouts and prevent them from doing their job of channeling water away from the house.

For starters, you will need a ladder long enough to reach the highest level of gutter, if you have a two-story house, for example. A twenty-foot extension ladder might prove good for this job. It is easy to store and practical. When working at heights, it is always a good safety idea to have a work partner there with you, if for no other reason than to hand you stuff.

These days a large percentage of new homes are built with aluminum or plastic gutters. These materials also are the choice of owners of older homes for replacement of existing gutters that are damaged beyond repair. They are durable, light, and easy to install in one of three ways: with long spikes and sleeve hangers, strap hangers, or bracket hangers. Some homes have gutters made of copper or wood, although wood is rare.

WOOD GUTTERS

Compared to plastic and aluminum, wood gutters are high maintenance, that is, a pain. Some houses have them today because the owners never got around to replacing them or they want them for aesthetic reasons. Whatever the reason, to protect the gutters from wood rot, they should be painted inside and out at least every two or three years. An asphalt roof paint is used for the inside of the tray and regular exterior house paint for the outside.

Planning for the job is very important, as a long stretch of dry weather (about one week) will be essential to do the job properly since the wood must be perfectly dry to be properly prepared.

1. **Make certain the ladder is resting on firm ground.**

2. Pull the rope on the ladder to hoist the extension to the desired height. The extension will lock in place on the appropriate rung of the ladder. It should extend at least two feet higher than the work area.

3. Do not overreach just to avoid getting down and moving the ladder. And don't try "hopping" the ladder every couple of feet, unless you're a trained circus act. Get down and move it. Keep your hips between the ladder rails. Grip the the ladder for support with one hand and clear out the gutter with the other.

4. Clear the debris from the inside tray, using a wire brush to scrape up any matter that is stuck to the wood.

5. Sand it smooth and clean.

6. Apply a coat of nonfiber asphalt roof paint, being careful not to let any drip on the exterior of the gutter since roof paint is impossible to clean up and will leach through regular exterior paint applied over it. Allow the roof paint application about two days to dry thoroughly and then apply one more coat.

VINYL, PLASTIC OR ALUMINUM

1. After cleaning away the heavy debris, use a garden hose to flush the gutter tray. Clear the downspout by inserting the hose directly in its opening and pushing it through to break up any jam, then flushing the channel with a full force of water.

2. Install a nylon mesh leaf strainer the length of the gutter to keep leaves from settling in the tray.

What? You want to install new gutters yourself?! Cool. Here's how you do it. **First,** decide what kind of gutter material you want to use: vinyl, plastic, or aluminum. If you are merely replacing a section be sure to replace with the same material, since there are different hangers used for one gutter material versus another. **Calculate** how much you will need. Gutters come in ten-foot lengths and are available in white, black, and brown. **Figure out** the type and number of hangers you will need against what is already there. Hangers should be installed every three feet. **Slip joint connectors** will be needed to join each section of gutter. **Offset elbows** come in a front, left, or right mount. Elbows are needed for the purpose of connecting the gutters to the downspouts and keeping the downspouts from resting against the house. Some vinyl and aluminum models of gutters have an end unit with a drop hole precut for the elbow and downspout connection. Otherwise, you will have to measure and cut the hole yourself.

Roof Safety Tips

Weather: Never go on the roof when it is raining, windy, or there is the threat of lightning. A wet roof is slick and treacherous, winds blow stronger higher up, and your body is a perfect lightning rod. Wait for dry, warm weather.

Beware of power lines and stay away from them.

Footwear: Avoid leather soles. Wear dry, soft-soled shoes. Athletic shoes work well.

Clothing: Wear loose, comfortable clothing with lots of pockets. Tuck in shirts and blouses. Flatten or button cuffs.

Plan ahead: Think about the tools and supplies you will be needing up top and load them in a bucket and your work apron. You'll want to eliminate any round-trips on the ladder and trekking across the roof.

Leave an extensively damaged roof to the care of a professional.

The Chimney

The dirt and soot produced by a wood-burning fireplace collects on the walls of the chimney and can cause a chimney fire if left unattended. It is important to have the chimney inspected annually and cleaned when necessary. Hiring a chimney sweep company may prove the most economical way. It is a messy job. They use heavy-duty vacuum equipment and will likely create less of a mess and do the job in less than half the time it might take the average homeowner. Ask the chimney sweep to

▶ **REAL MAN
TIP:**

A real man will offer to
climb the ladder first but he
will hold the ladder steady
if she insists on making the
trip up herself.

note the condition of the flue liner and report any cracks or damages to you. You will want to arrange to repair any chimney damage that is discovered as soon as possible.

While the chimney sweep company works mostly from the fireplace end, if you choose to do the task yourself, it will have to be done from the roof end. The company has the equipment to scrape the soot buildup from the flue and draw it down into the vacuum. You, on the other hand, will have to push and scrape. Don't do this to yourself. It is not worth it. Hire a chimney sweep!

SPARK ARRESTERS AND RAIN AND WIND GUARDS

Spark arresters are a good barrier against sparks and embers flying out of the chimney. They are made of a wire mesh that is saddled over the chimney flue. They are also good for preventing birds and other matter from getting into the fireplace.

Rain and wind guards come in several forms. Some are turbines that are inserted directly over the flue opening. Another type is simply a concrete slab that sits atop brick piers that rise six to twelve inches above the chimney opening.

Terms

Dry Well: An underground system for diverting water away from a house's foundation.

Fascia Board: The board that covers the joint between the eaves and the top of a house wall.

Flashing: Made of copper or other metal material, flashing protects the roof at its seams and joints, where leaks are most likely to occur. Flashing is found around chimneys, plumbing vents, and hips and valleys of the roof.

Flue: A part of a chimney that channels smoke and flame to the outer air.

Headers: A beam fitted at one side of an opening to support floor joists, studs, or rafters.

Hips: Where two parts of a roof join, creating a ridge seam.

Pitch: The slope or downward angle of an object.

Rafters: Parallel beams that support a roof.

Sheathing: Plywood or fiberboard material that provides the base for roof surface material.

Subroof: The framework of rafters that support a roof.

Valley: The elongated depression that forms when two slopes of a roof meet.

IF Moisture is a PROBLEM, try PLANTING PLANTS & SHRUBS with SHALLOW ROOT SYSTEMS Next To the FOUNDATION. They SOAK UP AN AMAZING AMOUNT of WATER.

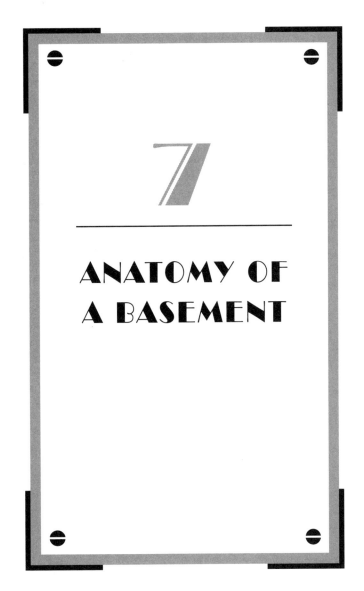

7

ANATOMY OF A BASEMENT

Basements in old houses get no respect. We treated ours like a ship's hold. The first year we lived in the house, we stored stuff in boxes piled in neat stacks on pallettes on the floor along the walls. But after a time nothing accounted for the way the family unceremoniously hurled its junk into the dark corners down there. The only rule was to maintain a path wide enough to maneuver unobstructed from the stairs to the washing machine and clothes dryer with a laundry basket in your hands. Make no mistake, the place where the washing machine and clothes dryer were was nothing as formal as a laundry room. It was just a spot where the two machines conveniently fit along a wall tucked out of the way in the rough-hewn cellar.

About five feet of the basement's height was subterranean. Its foundation walls were a twelve-inch thickness of large stones, and the floor was cold, functional concrete. The joists and beams that supported the house were huge, unglamorous, eight-by-eight wooden railroad ties. The builder had staged the beams on two-inch-thick concrete blocks and plopped them in odd points in the room—some with only a shoulder-and-a-half width between them—showing a total disregard for ambience and the possibility that somebody in the future might want to turn this make-do hole into a finished area of charming living space.

That's the way it was for me and still is for thousands of people who live in homes built before Dick Clark and *The American Bandstand* inspired the club basement era of the 1960s. Previously, paneled walls and carpeted floors were unheard of in a cellar, which is how that space was unprettily referred to in 1960 B.C. (before club).

This was the damp, dank, often dark, unlivable storage and utility space in the house. It was expected to get wet and moldy, and little was done to prevent those occurrences because homeowners did not regard the intruding moisture as an endangerment to vital appliances such as the furnace and hot water heater. There *were* no laundry machines.

But then along came the explosion in television sets, stereos, 45s, the Motown sound, and the discovery of a use for blue lightbulbs in the basement. The cellar was transformed into an entertainment center and an extension of the family living space. It worked fine as long as there was no rain. However, dampness that had been overlooked on the concrete floor of 1960 B.C. continued to do what dampness does and had to be wrung out of the shag carpets and mopped from under loosened floor tiles in the age of the club basement.

Water Water Everywhere

Today, moisture remains the most common basement problem that a homeowner faces whether or not the space is finished. Cracks in the walls or floor, clogged or nonexisting footing drains, nonexistent foundation wall waterproofing, improper grading, and just plain shoddy construction practices can contribute to water in the basement. And as long as homes have subterranean basements, water will always be an issue since the earth is water's natural habitat.

Some homes are built over springs, increasing the probability of water seepage in the basement. Moisture will intrude through cracks in the wall, and when the water table has risen high enough, water will soak upward through the concrete floor seeking its level, as the lesson goes, turning the basement into a well. However, with forethought, homeowners can anticipate and manage water seepage.

The Foundation

The foundation of a house has a formidable job. Not only must it hold up the entire house but it must act as a retaining wall to hold back the surrounding earth and protect the basement, if there is one, from the elements. The foundation walls can be made of stone, cinder block, concrete block, poured concrete, brick, or clay tile.

Foundation construction begins below ground level with a poured concrete footing around the perimeter of the house site to support and distribute the weight of the foundation wall and basement floor. The basement floor is concrete poured over a substructure of gravel or slag and sand filling. Basement floors are four inches or more in thickness. Expansion joints (spaces) are established at the base of the wall and the floor to allow for minor shifting and settling of the house. Drain tiles, which usually are pipes made of clay, should be laid along the footing of the exterior wall to divert water away from the house to the storm sewer or a dry well. Unfortunately, many times builders do not install drain tiles.

Anatomy of a Basement

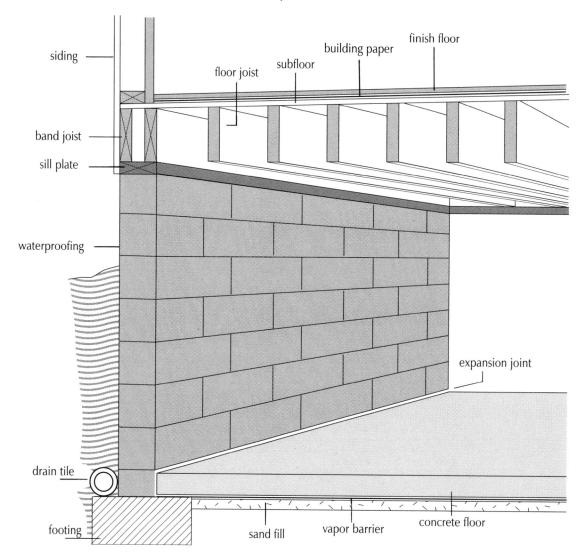

siding

floor joist

subfloor

building paper

finish floor

band joist

sill plate

waterproofing

expansion joint

drain tile

footing

sand fill

vapor barrier

concrete floor

Drain tiles also should be laid inside the basement under the floor and connected to a sump pump or storm drain.

Before gravel and earth is filled in, several coats of waterproofing compound and/or sheeting should be applied to the exterior foundation walls at least from ground level and below. However, sometimes builders don't apply even one layer of waterproofing, thus shortening the life of the foundation and guaranteeing a wet basement. A **good drainage** system is the first line of defense against water entering the house. A good system redirects water before it gets to the foundation. As you get to know your house the hard way—through repair necessities—you will make the sad discovery that there are many preventive steps that should have been taken with your house during construction that were not.

SO, WHERE'S THE WATER COMING FROM? AND WHY?

If the basement has a damp feel and smells musty, and if water beads on the pipes and appliances, condensation is the likely problem—warm air meeting cool air. The air in the basement usually is cooler than the air outside. So when the temperature heats up outside, a temperature imbalance occurs between the cool basement air inside and the warmer air outside. As a consequence, the basement air becomes humid and condensation forms. Other contributors to basement humidity are an unvented clothes dryer or the moist heat from the clothes washer or a basement shower. You can solve those problems by trying one or more of the following:

1. Venting the dryer to the outside of the house.

2. Opening basement windows for better ventilation.

3. Installing an exhaust fan in the basement.

4. Installing storm windows and keeping doors closed to prevent warm outside air from entering.

5. Investing in a dehumidifier.

Whichever you choose, do include insulating the hot and cold water pipes and heating pipes as well.

Water seeping through the basement wall and floor is a little more threatening than just a humid, musty smell. There are several possible sources. Roof **gutters** may be cluttered and overflowing, providing poor drainage. The **downspouts** may be dumping runoff toward the foundation of the house. Drains in **window wells** may be clogged. The ground **water table** may be high. The house may be constructed over a **spring,** or the soil may be **banked improperly** toward the house. Or it can be all of the above.

WHAT TO DO?

Start with the obvious.

Check drains in window wells for debris and check gutters and downspouts. **Leaks** can easily be spotted in gutters by looking up at them during a rainfall. Seal any joints that have separated. Adjust the slope of the gutters if need be.

Make sure downspouts are angled away from the house, that they are not dripping directly onto the ground but onto splashblocks.

Splashblocks should be on an incline away from the house and ideally connected to a dry well or storm drain.

Grade the soil so that it slopes away from the foundation of the house.

Set in a bed of plants and shrubs with shallow root systems next to the house foundation. They will soak up an amazing amount of water.

Patch cracks in walls and floors using a hydraulic cement patching compound. Hydraulic cement expands so that the repair itself will not crack. It also dries quickly in wet conditions. Prepare the crack for patching by chiseling it open just wide enough to allow the patch material to fit. Brush away loose concrete and dust. If you are making the repair while the wall is dry, dampen the crack slightly. Then use a trowel to force the cement compound into the space. After the compound has set, smooth it out with a wet trowel so that it is flush with the rest of the wall. Apply waterproofing material.

Sometimes the joint where the floor and the wall meet is not absolutely watertight and water may force its way through. Fill the joint with an epoxy patching mix following the mixing directions on the package. This job should be done during a dry spell, as epoxy will not adhere to wet surfaces.

Plug a leaking hole by cutting a little ledge in the hole and filling the hole with a quick-setting hydraulic cement. Mix it according to manufacturer's directions and form it into a carrot-shaped plug. When the material begins to stiffen, which should be in just a few minutes, press it into the hole like a cork and hold it in place with your hand or a trowel until it sets. Smooth the surface with a trowel before the plug has had time to completely harden.

Try **waterproofing** walls from the inside with asphalt or cement compounds made for masonry walls. Waterproofing material is designed to expand and harden when it enters the pores of a cinder block or concrete wall. The best bet for application and mixing is to follow the manufacturer's directions on the packaging. However, the procedure usually goes as follows:

Dampen the walls first by misting them with a garden hose. Although the wall should be wet, water should not be visibly clinging to it. With a brush or trowel **apply** the waterproofing materials only to the areas where seepage is a problem. Start at the bottom of the wall where the water

► CRACK
ALERT:

If a basement wall is bowing inward or contains horizontal or vertical cracks that are widening, the house has a structural problem. That will require the attention of a foundation expert.

pressure would be the greatest. Feather the material out to smooth edges. When the coating is dry to the touch, **dampen** the wall again and let it set overnight. When it has dried again, wet it down thoroughly with a garden hose and apply a second coat of waterproofing. **Two** coats are necessary at a minimum. **Note** that many waterproof mixes will not stick to painted walls. You will have to sand, wire brush, or sandblast the paint from the surface. **Epoxy and latex waterproofing** will not bond to wet surfaces. The surface must be completely dry before application.

However, if the basement floor constantly takes on water you may need to take more intrusive steps. You may need to install a **sump pump** or **drain tiles** in the interior of the basement. Both require digging up a portion of the basement floor. The **sump pump** is inserted into a pit in the lowest part of the basement floor and is hooked to the storm sewer or other device for channeling runoff away from the house. You need to choose a pump large enough to handle the subterranean water that collects beneath the floor. As the water level rises, a float activates a motor that pumps the water out. Talk with the experts at your home improvement center and find out what's involved before hiring someone to do the job.

Drain tiles are another way of diverting water from the basement. They are installed along the interior perimeter of the basement's foundation walls and are connected to the storm sewer or sump pump.

The builder may not have installed **exterior drain tiles** nor waterproofed the foundation walls. That job will require professional help. The ground next to the foundation wall must be excavated right down to the footing, which may be as deep as five or six feet. The earthen sides of the ditch must be secured to prevent a cave-in while working and the tile put in place. While the ground is excavated is an opportune time to assure that the foundation walls are waterproofed. It is a big job. If they have not been, hire a professional to do it.

WATERSOAKING SHRUBBERY

Hedges and other shrubbery planted around the periphery of a house are not just a matter of aesthetics. The greenery is a natural sponge for groundwater and thus an excellent first line of defense against leaky basements. Their shallow roots not only drink heavily but are nonthreatening to a house's foundation. (See Chapter 13 for more on the benefits of shrubbery and trees as natural wind barriers and water soakers for your property.)

▶ **MUSTY?**
MILDEW?

Fresh coffee beans set around the basement in brown paper bags will arrest those odors.

▶ **REAL MAN**
TIP:

A real man reads directions.

Terms

Drain Tiles: A perforated pipe installed along the exterior and interior footing of a foundation wall to channel water away from the foundation. Tiles installed under the basement floor usually are connected to a sump pump or the storm sewer.

Expansion Joint: Spacing created where two solid objects meet, as in a concrete wall and concrete floor. The joint, which is composed of material with expansive properties, acts as a buffer to prevent the two objects from cracking against each other as the foundation settles.

Footing: An enlargement at the lower end of a foundation wall to distribute the weight.

Parge or Parget: To apply plaster or waterproofing to an area.

Percolate: Testing the composition of the soil (percolate the soil) on a proposed building site to determine the best method and combination of materials for constructing the foundation.

Water Table: The water level in the ground.

Weep Pipe: A small pipe used to concentrate water from a leaking wall while repairs to the crack are being made.

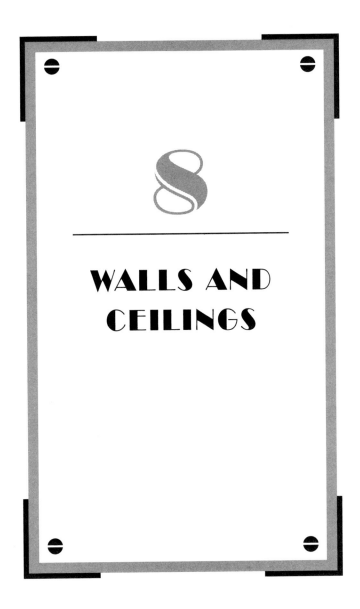

8

WALLS AND CEILINGS

The wallpaper was gorgeous. The pattern was a pale peach accented with a thin silvery stripe that repeated every three inches. Its overall satin finish gave it a look of wealth. It even had a name: Peachglo. It made a poor girl mistake herself for a princess.

However, her royal highness worked like a scullery maid the night before, singlehandedly applying the final panel of paper on the difficult section of wall that steeply angled up the stairway in what had become a way too long project. It was June and the job had been tackling me since February.

When I left for work that morning, I was utterly impressed. The job was done, it looked great, and I had done it all myself. I blew the newly covered walls a kiss as I left. I couldn't wait to get back home.

When I did return that evening I couldn't contain the giddiness of self-satisfaction as I unlocked the front door with images of my handiwork dancing in my head. I floated across the threshold and I am certain that I heard tiny lovebirds cozily cooing, crickets cricketing, and the little babbling brook—a requisite in such fantasy scenes—babbling away. I flipped on the light switch.

Yikes! The situation at the manor had regressed remarkably since morning. Much of the blessed just-too-cute wall covering had tumbled in a dead faint to the floor. One of the panels was still hanging on like a spent banana peel, clinging stupidly to the wall as if it was getting ready to jump but froze in place when it heard the door unlock. Seeing it was only me, it resumed its free fall onto the stairs.

You have nightmares about this kind of stuff. I didn't feel much like royalty. My brain was channel grazing and every station was showing Greta Garbo as the sickly Camille. She was dressed in a delicate peach look-of-wealth satin dressing gown with a thin silvery stripe every three inches. Camille was whispering something I could not make out.

When finally I found my voice, it sounded like Ricky Ricardo laughing at Lucy's latest harebrained scheme. I couldn't stop laughing. If you're going to do your own wallpapering, a sense of humor is critical. And if you don't come with any, rent some or a professional paperhanger.

I was caught in a netherworld of indecision. I had put too much time into this little job, told too many people about it, and had bragged all day about the perfect finish. Friends were coming by to check it out in a few days. What I wanted to do was go the only route a woman made insane by the sight could go and rip the remaining delicate peach stuff off of the walls and slap on some sensible off-white paint.

But the ego said "nah." Clearly, I had to do the job over again. But I didn't know what I had done wrong. I went over all the steps in my mind. I did everything right. Well, maybe not everything. Could it be that the shortcuts I took left out something really important? I didn't have to clean the wall first, did I? Holes don't need filling—that's what the wallpaper is for, right? You can put the new covering up over the old paper, can't you?

That's what the instructions said on the side of the can of paste I used, didn't it? If not there, surely I read it somewhere. I was in a hurry at the time, which was ridiculous considering that the walls had been sitting half started for four months. But during the weekend an irrepressible urge to bring the project to an end overcame me. The instruction sheet that came with the wallpaper was on the floor. I picked it up and sat on the hall steps to read it, carefully for the first time. Greta's asthmatic panting grew louder in my head. I now could make out what Camille was saying. She was gasping, "Wrong paste. Wrong paste."

Aha! Had I taken the instructions on the label seriously, I would have discovered that a "vinyl-to-vinyl" paste, which this paste was not, is necessary for covering over old paper. I would have learned that priming the walls, even ones with paper on them, is not the time waster I regarded it to be but an essential act. I saw those little directives about priming but I didn't have time for it and paste is paste, any kind will do. Of course, all wrong. The moral of this pathetic little tale is "Ignore the wall preparations and you can plan to do the job again real soon. Laziness will make you work."

Preparing Walls and Ceilings

Walls and ceilings are the skin of a room. Ones that are well toned and blemish free evoke a smile. Ones that are not provoke consternation whether the disfigurement is as insignificant as tiny picture nail holes in the wall or as serious as a sagging ceiling. Older homes with their well-worn parts provide a challenge. Escaping by selling the house and buying something new does not always free you from facing wall and ceiling repair at some point. It only delays the inevitable. Even if you buy a house fresh off the assembly line, you are not guaranteed no-maintenance, trouble-free interior surroundings.

Like children, new homes develop illnesses in infancy. Children get chicken pox. New homes suffer from PNS, or popped nail syndrome, an ailment which does to the surfaces of walls and ceilings what the pox does to a six-year-old's face. PNS begins its appearance in a house's first year as it undergoes settling pains. The expected shifting of the structure as it nestles into its foundation causes nails to wiggle themselves free from the studs and pop through the drywall. Floors and ceilings separate from the walls a bit, forming hairline cracks or worse, and caulking stretches out of place like a teenager growing over the summer. New and shiny does not mean trouble free.

Walls inside a house are either "bearing" or "nonbearing." Bearing walls provide the structural support for the floor above and the roof. Nonbearing walls are merely nonsupporting partitions. Prior to the 1950s, walls in residences were made chiefly of plaster. This tough material was mixed into a thick paste and generously slathered over a backing of wire mesh or wood strips, called laths. It dried fast and solid and experienced no shrinkage. Walls installed in houses built after the 1940s and through today are the fast and easy, dry kind known variously as wallboard or drywall or by its brand name, Sheetrock. It is used almost exclusively in residential and most commercial constructions today. Drywall comes in four-by-eight sheets and is nailed, screwed, or bonded with adhesive to a frame of studs and joists. From the viewpoint of a contractor interested in saving time and money, drywall does both far better than the installation of plaster walls.

Whatever your wall or ceiling may be, **DO NOT SKIP PREPARATION** whether you plan to cover it with wallpaper or paint it. Scrape away blemishes, patch cracks and holes, and apply a primer to seal the surface so that whatever you apply grips rather than soaks through. Prepping the surface can be time-consuming but it is not expendable. It is the pivotal step in the process you'll congratulate yourself for having taken.

Stripping Paint

Often, preparation includes stripping peeling, flaking paint on wooden windowsills and frames and moldings. Stripping paint back to the bare wood can be done with liquid stripping chemicals, the open flame of a butane torch, or an electric heat gun. I prefer the latter. It is faster, neater, and safer. Unlike the chemical strippers, a heat gun gets right to the bottom coat of paint. The coats peel up and fall in a dry heap that is easy to clean up. With chemical strippers, the peelings are wet and messy for some time before cleanup. The butane or open flame method has its dangers because the wood easily can be burned and working with an open flame indoors simply is not the safest choice to make. Whatever you choose as a paint stripper, be certain the room is ventilated. The fumes are toxic and can be overwhelming and dangerous in a closed space.

FIXING POPPED NAIL SYNDROME

Tools needed: wide trowel, four-to-six-inch putty knife, can opener, joint compound, scrap wood, fine sandpaper, paint brush or misting bottle.

1. Using a hammer, countersink the nail into the wall stud just hard enough so that it is slightly recessed and the hammer head leaves a slight impression or dimple in the wall. Take care not to hit hard enough to create a hole in the wall surface.

2. Fill the dimples with joint compound or wall patching material.

Fixing Popped Nail Syndrome

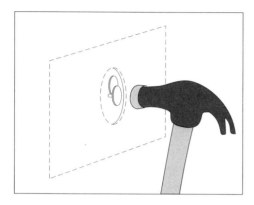

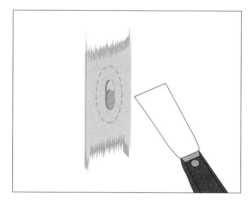

Countersink the nail into the wall, hitting it just hard enough so that it is silghtly recessed and the hammer leaves a slight impression or dimple. Fill the dimple with patching compound, scrape away excess and smooth out. Let dry for 24 hours, sand and paint.

Scrape away any excess, then feather the compound away from the patch point until it blends in smoothly with the rest of the wall.

3. Let dry for twenty-four hours. Use lightweight sanding paper to smooth the area. Prime the patch area with an oil-based primer and repaint the entire wall for an even look.

FILLING CRACKS

What you use to repair cracks in the walls or ceilings depends on what they are made of. If the wall's surface is made of paper, then the wall is drywall. If the wall is solid, chalky, and has no paper surface, it is plaster. Damaged plaster walls should be repaired with a plaster-based patching material. Drywall repairs do well with joint compound. Whatever your walls are made of, don't plan to do the repairs in a hurry. A good repair job needs at least a forty-eight hour curing period.

Drywall is comparatively easy to repair. Damage in drywall can be cut out, plugged with a scrap piece of drywall, and covered over with joint compound. This compound is available premixed or dry and is recommended for the inexperienced.

Some plaster walls and ceilings require a little more energy. They must be stripped back to the skeleton lath and built out again with a plaster-patching material. You can fill a small hole in plaster with plaster patch, spackle, or the joint compound used for drywall. However, a patch for a large hole in a plaster structure is best done with patching plaster, which is sold as a powder you will have to mix yourself. Adding plaster of Paris to the mixture helps it dry fast and hard and eliminates shrinkage.

HAIRLINE CRACKS IN PLASTER WALLS

1. Slightly enlarge the crack, using the tip of a file, a can opener, a screwdriver, or a putty knife to create a ledge on which the patching can sit. Brush away any loose bits of plaster and dust.

2. Moisten the crack with water, using a wet paintbrush or sprayer to assure a good bond.

3. Use a putty knife to fill the crack with patching material. Overlap on either side of the crack. Remove excess. Let dry for twenty-four hours. Apply another coat and wait another twenty-four hours.

4. Sand the area using a fine-grade sandpaper wrapped around a sanding block or a small block of two-by-four until smooth.

5. Apply a coat of primer to the patch area and its immediate surroundings. If necessary, paint the whole wall for even color.

REPAIRING A HOLE IN A PLASTER WALL

1. Remove loose plaster from around the hole.

2. Cut a piece of wire mesh screen larger than the hole and insert a length of wire through its center. Insert the mesh through the hole and fit it over the opening. Anchor it over the hole by tying a pencil to the length of wire and twisting it until the mesh is snugly in place.

3. Dampen the rim and inside the hole with water, using a paintbrush or misting bottle, then coat the edges of the hole with patching plaster.

4. Cover the hole, pushing a layer of plaster patch into and through the wire mesh. Let dry for twenty-four hours. Remove the pencil and untwist wire. Either let it drop behind the wall or pull it through.

5. Apply a second coat. Let dry twenty-four hours. Sand, prime with oil-based primer, and paint.

REPAIRING A HOLE IN WALLBOARD OR SHEETROCK

1. With a pencil and a straight edge, draw a box around the damaged area.

2. Drill a starter hole in each corner of the box and using a keyhole saw or sharp utility knife, cut out the damaged piece.

3. Create a brace from a length of one-by-two that is about four inches longer or wider than the hole. Insert the brace through the opening and position it flush against the back of the drywall so that it straddles the hole vertically or horizontally. Secure it with drywall screws to both sides of the opening.

4. Cut a patch the size of the hole from scrap wallboard.

5. Apply a coat of joint compound around the edges of the patch piece and fit it into place, pressing gently until the compound begins to bond.

6. Lay strips of self-sticking fiberglass drywall tape over the seams of the patch. Using a six-inch putty knife, spread joint compound over the patch area. Feather the compound out by gradually thinning the application away from the patch site until it is flat with the rest of the wall. Let dry twenty-four hours. Expect shrinkage. Apply a second coat using the same feathering procedure. Let dry another twenty-four hours, then sand the patched area, prime, and apply wall covering.

3 Step Repair Hole in Wall

Step 1

With a pencil and straight edge draw a box around the damaged area. Drill a starter hole in each corner of the box and cut out the damaged piece using a utility knife or keyhole saw.

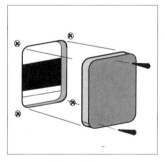

Step 2

Create a brace from a piece of 1 x 2 that is wider than the hole. Insert brace through the hole, position it flush against the back of the wall and secure it with drywall screws. Brace should straddle opening vertically or horizontally. Cut a patch the size of the opening from scrap wallboard.

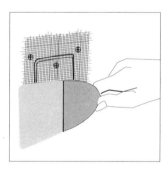

Step 3

Apply a coat of joint compound around edges of patch and fit into place. Lay drywall tape on seams of the patch. Spread compound over patch area, feather, let dry 24 hours. Apply second coat, let dry, sand, prime and paint entire wall for uniformity.

Get a Good Bucket of Paint

"Only the rich can afford to buy cheap paint," goes the saying among professional painters. Cheap paint guarantees repeated do-overs.

Like any other product, there's good paint and bad paint. The main ingredients in a gallon of paint are pigment, resins, and chalks. Application, washability, wearability, and color retention are factors to consider.

Too much of one ingredient and not enough of another marks the difference between a good gallon and a bad one. Cheap paint, like a cheap hamburger, is loaded with fillers and chalks. Also, the level of a manufacturer's vigilance over quality control from batch to batch determines the final product. When selecting paint, think about its long-term durability. It may be cheaper and covers well in its initial application but will it wear well? Or will it chalk your clothes when you brush up against it? Can you wash stains off of it without dulling the finish? In the long run, it's better to invest a little more in a good gallon.

Where to Buy Paint

Home improvement stores are popular as one-stop shops for the home but caution should be exercised when buying paint there. An experienced painter may be assigned to the department, but if he or she is off that day you may end up getting advice from, perhaps, a carpenter who may be excellent at carpentry but no better than you at painting.

While I buy nearly every other home repair and maintenance item at these supermarket stores, I've taken to buying my paint at quality independent paint stores. They know paint. All they sell is paint and painting supplies. The people there are trained to answer questions, and there are plenty of questions that go along with a gallon of paint. Oftentimes, we don't think of them ourselves, and that's where the paint professional's expertise comes in. If they are any good, they will raise the questions. It might mean delaying your purchase until you can get such answers as what kind of paint is already on the wall? A glossy, semigloss, or flat paint or a light or dark color? Once again, the biggest painting mistakes begin with failure to prepare the surface and select the appropriate paint. The actual painting is the easy part.

Doing It

You've cleaned the walls, scraped off peeling, flaking, blistered paint, patched the holes, removed switch and receptacle covers, detached the door knobs, and covered or removed your favorite ceiling light fixture. Apply masking tape to the wall-side edges of doorframes and moldings to protect them. There is a painter's edging tape that is lightly glued. It removes easily without leaving the glue backing or damaging the surface it is covering.

If you are painting the entire room, paint the ceiling first, then the walls, the trim next, then the doors and windows.

Paint Tools

Checklist: Roller, trim brush or roller, masking tape, edger.

Brushes

Large does not make the job go faster, only sloppier. A three- or four-inch brush is big enough for large areas if you are going to do the entire job

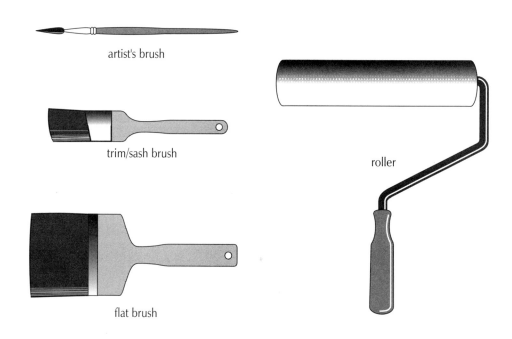

artist's brush

trim/sash brush

flat brush

roller

with a brush. A couple of trim or sash brushes of one to one and a half inches and two and two and a half inches are sufficient. A good brush holds more paint and allows you to apply the paint smoothly and effortlessly. Brush bristles are made with natural or man-made fibers. They should not pull free when tugged. Each bristle should be split or flagged at the tip, and should fan out when pressed against a surface and spring back to shape when released.

Rollers

Rollers are both fast and neat. Roller covers come in varying lengths, fabrics, and naps. A width of seven or nine inches is good for the average room. Smaller sizes are available for small spaces such as window trim and moldings, although you may find that small trim brushes are easier to handle in these instances. Special-purpose rollers are available for painting in corners and edging, and there are special-effect covers for textured and designer looks. Longer naps are used on masonry and other bumpy surfaces.

Select the roller cover based on the paint being used as well as the surface. Lamb's wool is good with oil-based or alkyd paints, but latex paint causes the wool to mat. Mohair rollers are good for use with enamel or any type of flat interior paint.

Rolling It Out

Begin by painting the corners and wall area nearest the ceiling, using a brush or corner roller. Do not heavily saturate the brush or roller. Wet only the edge of a brush. Do not submerge the roller in the paint. Get a broad edge wet and roll the roller along the shallow portion of the paint tray to remove excess paint. Roll the paint onto the main wall in a crisscross. Smooth the paint by going over the area using up-and-down strokes.

If the ceiling is not to be painted at all or is to be painted a color different from the walls, you can get a clean joint by using a brush and the "cutting in" technique in which you **push** rather than swath the paint. Dab paint on a small area of the wall close to the ceiling and use the edge of the brush to gently **push** the paint toward the seam joining the wall and ceiling.

For door and window frames and molding, use a small trim brush and take your time.

Let Someone Else Do It?

You'd rather hire a painter. That's okay. However, there are painters and there are painters—commercial, industrial, and residential. Be aware that their talents are not necessarily interchangeable. Mr. or Ms. Industrial may be the finest painter of bridges in the universe. However, the broad-brush technique for bridge painting won't do in your dining room where subtle trim work can make or break the look. Industrial and commercial painters usually do not make good residential painters, as they lack the fine-art temperament. Of course, there are exceptions to the rule. But a good rule of thumb is if the painter's credentials boast the San Francisco Bay Bridge, pass.

Just like choosing a gallon of paint, you can go cheap or you can go expensive when selecting a painter. Cheap is not necessarily a bad choice, but you set yourself up for problems when you hinge the choice solely on cost. Investigate. For instance, you bring two companies in to bid on the job of painting your porch and the outside window frames of your house. One charges $10 an hour and the other charges $20. Of course, $10 is a cheap price. To save money, you lean toward Mr. $10. Now, just how cheap is this price? You learn through his previous clients that Mr. $10 can do the job in a few hours. But he is a paint slob who thinks a drop cloth is a rag that's fallen out of his back pocket. With no preparation to the paint site, he slops a ten-inch brush on a two-inch frame, paint chips and all, leaving you with a narrower point of view. When he's done you've got paint on the azalea bushes and the car, which was twenty yards away in the driveway, and he does minimal cleanup. If you hire this guy, the cheap price would be a cheap job that in the end would prove pretty expensive.

Mr. $20-an-hour's previous customers say he takes as long as two days to do the work. But no wonder: He scrapes the loose paint away first, uses

WALLS AND
CEILINGS

► REAL MAN
TIP:

A real man wears work
gloves and goggles.

the proper-sized brushes, and utilizes a drop cloth and a wipe rag and knows which one to apply where. In the long run he clearly is the better choice.

Nobody will ever say they *want* a cheap job. What we mean is we want a good job for a cheap price. Of course, what we really want is perfection, a pipe dream that we seek at the lowest price. But we end up settling for adequate because that may be all we can get in this world.

If you decide to hire an adequate painter, you should supply the paint and let your selection be guided by where the paint is being applied: outside, inside, in a highly traveled area or one constantly exposed to heavy moisture, or on drywall or masonry. Discuss the application thoroughly with a paint expert first before engaging a painter. Then have that same discussion with the painter you select to find out how he or she plans to proceed.

9

FLOORS AND DOORS

I installed wall-to-wall carpet in my entry hallway once and cut the telephone line while I was at it. I had become so overwhelmed with pride over doing a good job of something I had never attempted before that I stopped paying attention to the job itself. I was marveling at how my folding and tamping the edges of the rug gave it the nice, professionally installed look I once would have paid for. That's when I accidentally sliced the telephone wire with my utility knife. The line was tacked along the base of the attic steps where I was trimming excess carpet, but some of the line had pulled loose from its track, and as I cut into the carpet I cut the wire. I didn't realize what I had done until I tried dialing out. I never would have thought of installing the carpeting myself except I couldn't grasp the concept of paying a $90 installation charge for a $70 "piece a rug," as my mother would have said. My mind told me "You can do this." And so I did. All that was involved was some two-sided carpet tape, a tape measure, a sharp utility knife, patience, and

Anatomy of a Stairway

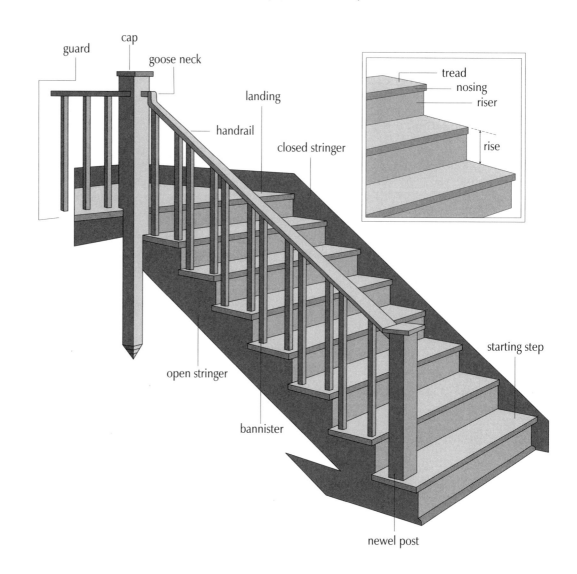

guard

cap

goose neck

landing

handrail

closed stringer

tread

nosing

riser

rise

open stringer

bannister

starting step

newel post

When working on wood flooring, always drill a pilot hole first. The hole should be smaller than the size of the nail to be used and always drilled at an angle, for a better grip. Failure to predrill the nail hole could result in split wood.

my very own common sense. I finished off the job with brass thresholds at the entrances to the bedrooms to give the hallway the look of professionalism I had hoped to achieve. Then I sat down and wrote myself a check for $90. You might discover that saving money is all the motivation you will ever need to attempt to do a job yourself.

Quieting Squeaky Floors and Steps

Good hardwood floors give an air of charm to a house. But sooner or later even the most solidly laid wood floors squeak and you'll need to do something. And throwing a carpet over the floor is not the answer. You must fix the squeak first.

You would squeak too if you were constantly under pressure. The sound generally is caused by two boards rubbing against each other. Even the best wood flooring eventually delivers up a squeal. Since wood is alive, it responds to atmospheric changes—swelling when it is humid and shrinking when the air is dry. Floorboards shift, warp, and split. Typically, the joists warp, bowing away from the floorboards they support above, causing a squeak when someone walks by. Sometimes the joists have dried out. Inadequate nailing of the floorboards or subfloor to the joists also could be the problem; just plain cheap flooring could be another, or major structural damage below could be yet another. With a little investigation you will figure out which is which.

The ideal way to silence a squeaky floor or step is from underneath. But if you do not have access from the underside, no problem—it can be done from above.

Carpeted Floors

Pull back the rug and check the flooring for warping or loose nails. With some rooms that have wall-to-wall carpeting, there is an underlayment of plywood beneath the padding. Check for warping in the squeak area. Drill pilot holes in the underlayment in the area of the squeak, then drive in spiral shanked flooring nails to resecure it to the joists below.

Hardwood Floors

Drill pilot holes at an angle and drive in flooring nails. Countersink the nail head by driving the nail so that its head sits just beneath the surface of the floorboard and fill the space with wood putty.

Wood Floors

WORKING BENEATH THE SQUEAK

Pinpointing some weaknesses requires at least two people—one person to walk on the squeaking area and the other in the basement checking the flooring's underside for corresponding movement. Sometimes, there is a gap between the joist and subfloor boards that causes the noises. If the gap is slight, it can be corrected by inserting a shim in the space. A shim is merely a thin sliver of wood that you can create from scrap wood. Gently wedge the shim into the space between the joists and the subfloor to prevent movement. Easy does it. You just want to fill the space. Tap the shim in too hard and you will widen the gap, raise the floor, and aggravate the problem.

Floor Squeaks

1.
From beneath floor insert
wood shingle (shim)
between the subfloor & the
joist.

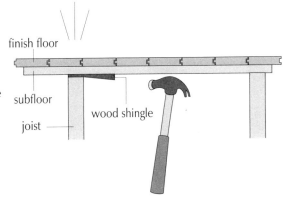

finish floor

subfloor

joist

wood shingle

2.
Drive a screw through
subfloor and floorboard to
stabilize shifting boards.

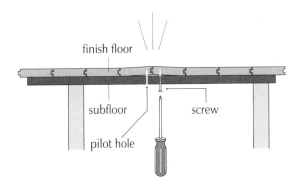

finish floor

subfloor

pilot hole

screw

3.
Nail down the squeaking
boards.

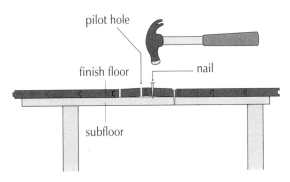

pilot hole

finish floor

nail

subfloor

Reinforcing and Bridging Joists

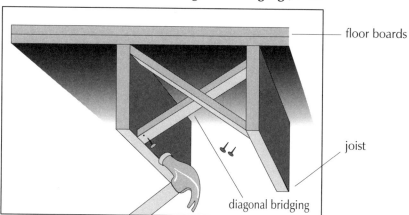

floor boards

joist

diagonal bridging

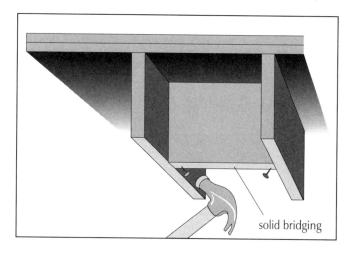

solid bridging

SAGGING JOIST

If the gap caused by a warped joist is wide enough, it won't provide adequate support and could cause a dip in the flooring. A shim won't do in this case. To fix this, wedge a piece of one-by-four against the joist and against the subfloor to bridge the gap. Firmly prop the one-by-four in place using a two-by-four as shown and nail or screw the one-by-four to the joist.

SHIFTING JOISTS

Squeaking across a large area indicates that the joists are shifting. Nail all loose diagonal bridging. If you must add bridging, make the addition a real tight fit between the adjoining joists. Tap it into place, then secure it with nails that have been driven in toenail fashion, that is, at an angle rather than straight down.

A SAGGING FLOOR

The dining- and living-room floors in my first house not only squeaked but also sagged at the threshold, making part of the floor appear to have a huge hump. The sagging occurred because a bright light who once owned the house decided to remove a support beam in the basement. Apparently it got in the way of a decorating scheme. Support beams exist for a very important, obvious reason. Without the support the floor will drop. In fact, the whole house would come tumbling through.

Sagging in the flooring of the first floor of a house will critically affect every floor above it and the roof as well. Cracks in the walls and ceilings, roof leaks, and sticking doors and windows all are the result of sagging floors.

CORRECTING THE SAGS: REINFORCING JOISTS

Begin in the basement by installing support under the joists. Lifting a sagging floor will take anywhere from several days to several weeks depending on how badly the floor is sagging. This process *must* not be rushed. It must be done gradually, else serious damage can be done to the house.

The way to lift a sagging floor is to use a house jack. These can be rented or purchased, depending on whether the jack is to be kept in place permanently or temporarily until permanent support beams are installed.

One type of jack is a steel device that has a four-by-four vertical post extender. The task will require two four-by-four beams and one four-by-eight. Start by placing one four-by-four beam on the basement floor underneath the sagging area as a base for the jack. The beam will also protect the concrete floor from cracking under pressure as the joists are elevated. The second four-by-four is the vertical post extender. The four-by-eight fits horizontally across the extender and placed directly under

Adjustable Jack Post

top plate

removable
jack handle
in height
adjustment nut

heavy Acme
screw threads

upper post with
height adjustment holes

adjustment pin
and support collar

lower stationary post

bottom plate

minimum size
solid concrete
foundation:

24" square,
12" deep

Sagging Floor

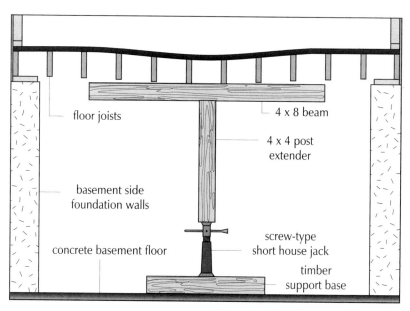

floor joists

4 x 8 beam

4 x 4 post
extender

basement side
foundation walls

concrete basement floor

screw-type
short house jack

timber
support base

Once in place, turn jack handle until there's resistance. Leave it for 24 hours. After 24 hours turn jack handle no more than 1/4 turn. Do this every 24 hours until floor is pushed back in place.

the sagging joists. It should be at least the length of the sag area. Once all is in place, turn the jack handle until there's resistance. Leave the project for at least twenty-four hours. During that time the joists gradually are being pushed back into place and made limber, the way muscles are stretched slowly to prevent injury. Forcing the lift could damage the entire house.

After twenty-four hours turn the jack handle **no more than a quarter turn,** even if it feels easy. Do this for as many days or weeks as it takes to push the floor back in place.

An adjustable steel jack post is another choice for permanent fixes. It can be left in place. The lift principle is the same. Gradually!

REPLACING DAMAGED FLOORBOARDS

Some homeowners' idea of taking care of a hardwood floor problems is to cover it up with tile. When I pulled up the worn tile on the hallway floor of my old house, beneath it lay wonderful hardwood flooring. Some of the boards needed replacing, but for the most part the floor was in good condition.

Wood floors may be either boards that are glued and nailed in place or tongue and groove. Replacement and repair of individual boards or sections is fairly easy.

Using a hammer and sharp chisel carefully split the defective board along the grain and pry out the pieces. Carefully measure the opening and cut a replacement to fit.

Put the board in place and tap it down firmly, using a hammer and a block of wood to protect the new surface from marring. Fill any narrow gaps with wood putty. If the gap is *that* big, recut the board for a better fit.

Secure in place with finishing nails, which are thin nails with a small head. Drill pilot holes at the ends and along the sides of the board. Countersink the nail heads and fill the holes and seams with color-matched wood putty.

For parquet floors, gently hammer and chisel the parquet tile until it is broken free. Clean the area and reseat the replacement tile.

QUIETING SQUEAKY STEPS: TREADS AND RISERS

Steps squeak for the same reason wood floors squeak. Wood is rubbing against wood. In the case of steps, the tread rubs against the riser at the front end, back end, or both. The steps in my old house used to squeak, but we did nothing about them. We pretended they were a natural alarm for burglars or for when we'd gone to bed and the kids overstayed their curfew. Of course, we could never go to bed while the kids were not home. And once we installed that ear-splitting security system in the house, we had no more pretexts for not silencing the squeaks. Yet we never did. Although the noise remained, we simply never heard it anymore.

For squeaks at the front end of the tread, have someone stand on the offending step as you drive a few finishing nails into the front edge of the tread. Drill pilot holes first to avoid splitting the wood. Drive in the finishing nails.

Steps that talk from the back are caused by gaps. Fill the gap with a few shims or wedges of scrap wood. Coat the shims with wood glue and tap them into the gap between the riser and the tread. If you have access to the underside of the steps you can do a more cosmetically pleasing repair. You'll need two small blocks of one-by-two or two-by-two. Drill pilot holes through the blocks and apply wood glue to the two surfaces that will make contact to the riser and the tread. Fit the block snugly against the step and the riser and secure it in place with screws. Done.

Patching Carpet Linoleum

No, don't rip up all of the linoleum because a portion of it has a burn in it. Patch it. Get a piece of the same pattern and material larger than the damaged area.

Tape the patch piece over the damaged section. Make certain that the pattern is a precise match. Using a straight edge as a guide and a utility knife with a sharp blade, cut through all thicknesses of the patch and the damaged section.

Set aside the patch and lift out the damaged section. Thoroughly scrape away the adhesive from the exposed floor. Apply tile adhesive to the underside of the patch and position it in place. Clean up excess adhesive immediately. Weight down the patch area until the adhesive dries.

REPLACING DAMAGED VINYL TILES

Cover the damaged tile with a wet cloth and run a warm iron across it a few times to soften up the adhesive. Slash the tile in the middle with a sharp utility knife and pry it up with a hammer and chisel. Take care not to damage adjacent tiles. Scrape out old adhesive. Coat the replacement tile with adhesive. If the tile feels a little stiff, soften it up by placing a wet cloth on it and passing a warm iron over it a few times. Apply the adhesive to the back of the tile using a notched trowel. Line up the tile and insert it in place. **Press,** do not **slide** the tile into place. Clean up sediment immediately.

REGROUTING TILE

Very often the grout will deteriorate before the tile it surrounds. To replace loose or damaged grout carefully chip out the old grout with a ham-

Patching Carpet Linoleum

Step 1

Tape a patch of the same pattern and larger than the damage over the damaged area. With a utility knife and straight edge cut through all thicknesses.

Step 2

Set aside the patch and lift out the damaged section. Scrape away adhesive from floor. Apply fresh adhesive to back of patch, position and press into place.

► **TIPS:**

Install the slot in the thickest portion of the door. For hollow-core doors, a metal sleeve should be inserted between the inside and outside slot plates to prevent mail from falling into the hollow. Tools: keyhole saw, tape measure, screwdriver, pencil.

mer and cold chisel. Hold the chisel at an angle and take care not to harm the tiles. When the old grout is out, clean the particles from the joints with a stiff-bristled brush and a vacuum. Use a sponge to fill the joints with grout. (Color pigment can be added to the new grout to match the tile.) Wipe away any excess grout with a sponge.

Doors

INSTALLING A MAIL SLOT

Whenever I was away for days at a time, my neighbor's daughter would retrieve my mail from my box and hold it for me until I returned home. However, when I forgot to tell her I was going away the mail collected in the box. I might as well have put a sign on the porch: "HEY THIEVES! NOBODY'S HOME."

Never one who liked imposing on others, I decided to put a mail slot in my front door. It was one of the best decisions I ever made.

The good news is most mail slot designs come with a template in the package and excellent illustrated directions. To determine the size of the opening you will need, lay the template against the door and trace the outline with a pencil. Drill holes at each of the four corners of the outline and use a keyhole saw to cut out the opening. Insert the hollow door sleeve (not necessary for solid doors) and the mail slot and bolt in place with the inside and outside facing plates. And that's that.

INSTALLING A PEEPHOLE

Tools: drill, pencil, tape measure, coin.

Peepholes come in a few style selections. One of the best peepholes has a 190-degree angle viewer. It gives you a frog's eye view of objects that are on the periphery. Someone trying to hide in a corner of the door will be spotted. The directions that come on the packaging are straightforward. Using a pencil, mark the position on the door for the peephole. Make a half-inch hole using a half-inch drill bit. On the outside of the door insert one part of the viewer in the hole. Fasten it to the door by screwing on the viewing piece from the inside of the door. Use a coin to tighten the viewing piece in place. Done.

REPLACING OR INSTALLING A LOCK

I tried this. I am no good at it and have no personal experience to share that will help make it simple for anyone else to do. Actually, replacing or installing a lock can be easy if the conditions are ideal. But there are so many variables with doors and their locks. Few people have the ideal door condition. There's always something just a little unique about your particular door and lock assembly. I'm not an alarmist, just a realist. None of this is to say you should not try to work the lock yourself. You should at least try. These days lock manufacturers try to help make it easier to use their products by including easy-to-follow language and illustrations in the packaging. I would refer you to that.

The most critical—and ultimately vexing—part of working with door locks, particularly on doors that never had a lock before, is getting the door cylinder properly aligned with the strike plate and latch and making the right-sized holes for the knobs and latch. Smart lock manufacturers have included a paper template in the lock kit packaging to assist in making accurate alignment. You position the template on the body and face of the door where the knob and latch are to go and mark the positions with a pencil. Install the knob and latch and then close the door to line up the latch where the strike plate would go on the doorjamb.

Another aid that lock manufacturers provide is the brass cover-up or trim plate. These are especially useful for covering over old mounting holes on the body of the door and the long vertical recess on the face of the door designed to hold the assembly for a mortise lock. These locks were a standard issue at one time but are seldom if ever found in new housing construction. Cylindrical locks are more common in new construction. They take up less space on the door and are far easier to replace.

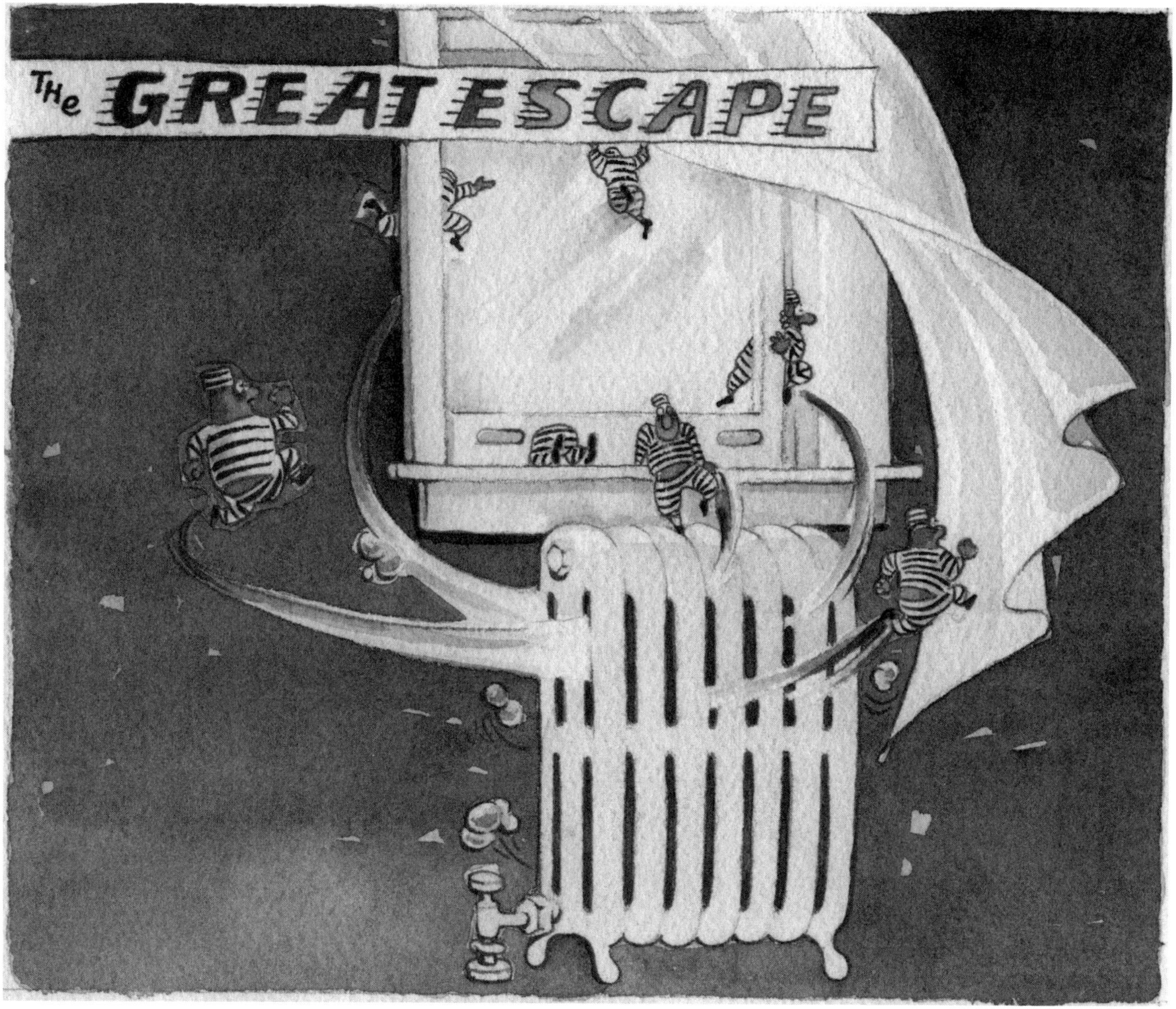
THe GREAT ESCAPE

10

WINDOWS

Every winter certain houses in my neighborhood developed that Saran Wrap look. That's the look windows get when their owners encase them in plastic. The idea is to keep the cold air out. Some people don't care what their plastic jobs look like on the outside as long as it means the inside is warm. They seal up the windows using quadruple layers of plastic bags saved from the dry cleaners revealing a callous disregard for curb appeal! I admit to having used plastic from the dry cleaner one year. It was a financial emergency. From the outside, the windows made the house look uncared for. Inside, the plastic was invisible, hidden behind window treatments. However, the air pocket that developed between the window and the plastic sheeting created a canopy-type bulge that made the drapes look like they were moments away from giving birth. But without the plastic the house was much colder. I considered buying replacement windows once but nixed the idea because it was too costly. And then I learned that replacement windows don't necessarily remedy the problem anyway. Of course, many of us wouldn't get this news flash until after we'd spent a winter with our new expensive windows that we had to wrap in plastic sheeting.

Being cash poor, I yielded to my hyperactive imagination. I put thin insulation foam in the side casing of some of the windows, packing in just enough layers to allow the weighted cord assembly housed inside the casing to move freely. Along with weather-stripping the windows, packing the casing helped reduce a great deal of the indoor chill that was coming through the jamb and molding.

About that chill. We indoor dwellers tend to think about the winter chill as the cold coming in. Often, the outside cold does leak in through the subtle and not-so-subtle openings in the window and under and around doors. But when you stand in front of a window and it feels like it is radiating cold, what actually is happening is the heat inside the house is escaping through the glass. That's an interesting concept when you realize that being cold is a two-way street.

The gains and losses of both heat and cold can be limited by the kind of windows you have. When you get to the point of replacing your old wooden windows remember that new isn't necessarily the main ingredient for better. Consider the layers of glazing. The more the merrier. Double-glazed windows limit heat gains and losses by using air as an insulator. The windows are composed of two panes with air sandwiched between them. Insulated windows are way better than putting up plastic wrap, drapes, and venetian blinds on the single-glazed version, which is what most of old homes have. However, if the window is installed carelessly, air can seep past the installation points and defeat the purpose of the purchase.

If it's storm windows you are going after, be certain they are installed with a tight fit to provide that extra thickness of insulation you are looking for. Obviously, single-layer windows are the least effective against cold and heat. But if that's what you have, go with the Saran Wrap until you can do better.

Double-Hung Windows

Double-hung windows are two sashes that slide past each other, providing an opening at the top and an opening at the bottom. These types of windows offer the best ventilation so that rising hot air can escape out of the window rather than linger at the ceiling. Fresh air blows in through the window's bottom half.

The movement of double-hung windows is controlled by pulleys with weighted cords made of rope or chains. Many double-hung windows are made of aluminum, but wood remains the most popular material.

LOOSENING UP A TIGHT SASH

From time to time double-hung windows will stick for a variety of reasons. Humidity may cause the wood to swell, weather stripping is too snug, paint chips and dirt may accumulate in the sash channel, or the window may be painted shut.

If **humidity** is the culprit, place a small block of wood in the sash channel between the stops and tap it with a hammer. This should spread the stops so that the sash has a little more room to move. Sanding the sash along its sides will also loosen things up a bit.

Weather stripping that is too snug can stop a sash in its tracks. Remove the stripping, then press it back in, repositioning it until the problem is solved.

Clean **dirt and paint chips** from the channel and lubricate it by rubbing a bar of soap along the path.

Double-Hung Window

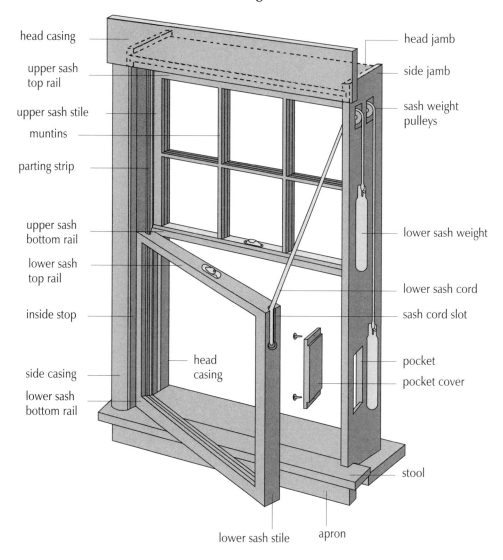

head casing

upper sash top rail

upper sash stile

muntins

parting strip

upper sash bottom rail

lower sash top rail

inside stop

side casing

lower sash bottom rail

head casing

lower sash stile

apron

head jamb

side jamb

sash weight pulleys

lower sash weight

lower sash cord

sash cord slot

pocket

pocket cover

stool

Break a paint seal by wedging a wide-blade putty knife between the sash and the inside stop at various points around the window and gently tap the knife handle with a hammer. Do not use a screwdriver or pointy tool, as either could damage the wood. No luck? If the window is accessible from the outside, insert a pry bar between the windowsill and the bottom rail of the sash and apply pressure upward. Try at several points along the windowsill. That should free it. Try the pry bar from the inside if the window is only accessible from inside.

TIGHTENING UP A LOOSE SASH

A loose sash means air will leak through the window. The situation is easily remedied by repositioning the window stops (molding) so that they snuggle closer to the sash.

1. Check to see how the stops are held in place, with nails or screws. Remove the screws first. If nails have been used, pry off the stops, being careful not to make big movements that could break the wood.

2. Chisel off any paint that has built up on the sash, the molding, and parting strip. Sand and rub them with bar soap or paraffin.

3. Replace the stops on the side jamb, adjusting them close enough to the sash to eliminate the play in the window but far enough back to allow the window to move freely.

REPLACING THE SASH CORD

The sash cords in most old houses are made of clothesline, which eventually becomes frayed and breaks. It is best to replace these ropes with a more durable chain link when the time arrives for a replacement.

Replacing a Sash Cord

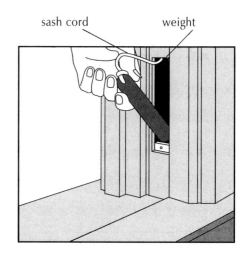

1. Using a putty knife, remove the inside moldings from both sides of the window.

2. Raise the bottom sash just high enough to swing one side of it clear of the window stool (sill).

3. Raise the weight by pulling the cord down. With the weight suspended in the air, free the cord from the sash. The cord is either nailed or hooked into a recess on the side of the sash.

4. Slacken the cord and let the weight down as far as it will go. Unscrew the access panel on the window jamb and remove the weight.

5. Feed one end of the chain over the pulley and let it drop down until you can see it by the access panel. Insert a long nail through one of the links at the other end of the chain to prevent it from dropping behind the jamb.

6. Secure the chain to the sash weight with wire or a small C-shaped hook.

7. Attach the other end of the chain to the sash and adjust the chain's length so that the weight will hang about three inches above the stool when the sash is fully raised.

8. Reseat the sash and window moldings.

Make a routine of vacuuming and cleaning the tracks of sliding doors and windows. Debris collects there as a matter of course. By regularly maintaining the tracks you can spot potential trouble before it becomes a real problem.

REPLACING A WINDOWPANE

Eventually every homeowner is faced with a broken windowpane. The repair job is so simple that skilled labor won't make house calls. It's not worth their time. If they do agree to come it will cost way more than the job is worth. Although simple, making the repair can result in serious cuts from tiny pieces of glass that you seldom see before you feel them. Then there's the matter of transporting the replacement sheet of glass. The exposed border has a rapier edge, and due diligence is a must while handling.

If you choose to do this repair yourself, a pair of thick gloves is a must. However, I discovered there is a superior option for getting the job done that limits the risk of injury and is even more cost- and time-effective than doing it yourself, especially if you're a first-timer. That's the one I'll tell you about.

Discover the small neighborhood hardware stores and glass shops. Most specialize in these repairs and do them cheaply and quickly—often, while you wait—if you bring the window sash to them. Ask if you can observe how the repair is done and part the curtain on one more home repair mystery without doing it yourself. This up-close and personal touch is one of the few remaining edges the old-fashioned hardware store has on the huge home superstores, some of which typically do not provide this service.

Removing the Window Sash

You will need to remove the inside stop or molding strip that runs vertically on either side of the sash. To do this, use the blade of a putty knife and gently pry away the molding, which is most likely nailed in place. Pry at several points along the molding strip to loosen it to prevent damage to the wood.

Then, lift the sash up slightly so that it clears the windowsill and turn one side toward you so that where the sash cord is connected to the sash is visible. The cord is made of either chain or rope. One end of the cord is nailed into the side of the sash and the other end is inside the jamb with a hunk of weight tied to its end. The weight keeps the window balanced when it is opened and closed.

Grab a length of the weighted cord and hold firmly as you unhook the end attached to the sash. **Do not let go,** else the weighted cord will disappear behind the jamb. Prevent this disappearing act by nailing the knotted end to the window frame. Do the same on the other side and remove the sash. Now, off to the store with you.

MENDING WINDOW SCREENS

It is amazing how little flying critters find their way through the tiniest tear in the window screen. Often the hole is so tiny we don't do anything

► REAL MAN
TIP:

A real man admits when he is lost.

Patching a Screen (Metal)

1.

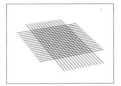

2.

3.

1. After trimming damaged area to a neat square, cut a patch from a piece of similar screening. Cut the patch larger than the damaged area.

2. Unravel strands on all of the edges of patch. Bend the strands and insert the wires through the mesh of the screen.

3. Bend wires of patch back onto screen to hold in place.

about it aside from wondering out loud, "How are those bugs getting in here?" When the tear is more noticeable we slap Scotch Tape over it, swearing we'll make a permanent repair "this weekend." Of course, "this weekend" never arrives mainly because we think it is a huge job and are not certain what to do. It's simple.

You can mend small tears in fiberglass or metal screens with a clear silicone glue. Dab it on and let it dry, then dab on another layer. The clear glue used for press-on fingernails is good if you have any around, although clear nail polish is not a good fix as it does not provide a strong bond.

Don't throw away that old screening. You can use strands of it as darning thread to repair holes in screens you want to keep.

Large holes will require a patch job. Trim the damaged area to a neat square or rectangle, with no frayed edges. From a piece of similar screening, cut a patch that is larger than the area to be repaired.

For **metal** screening, unravel strands on each edge of the patch. Bend the strands and insert the wires through the mesh of the screen. Bend the wires of the patch back on the screening to hold the patch in place.

For **fiberglass** screen, cut a patch from scrap fiberglass screening and simply glue it on with clear silicone, epoxy, or an acetone-type glue.

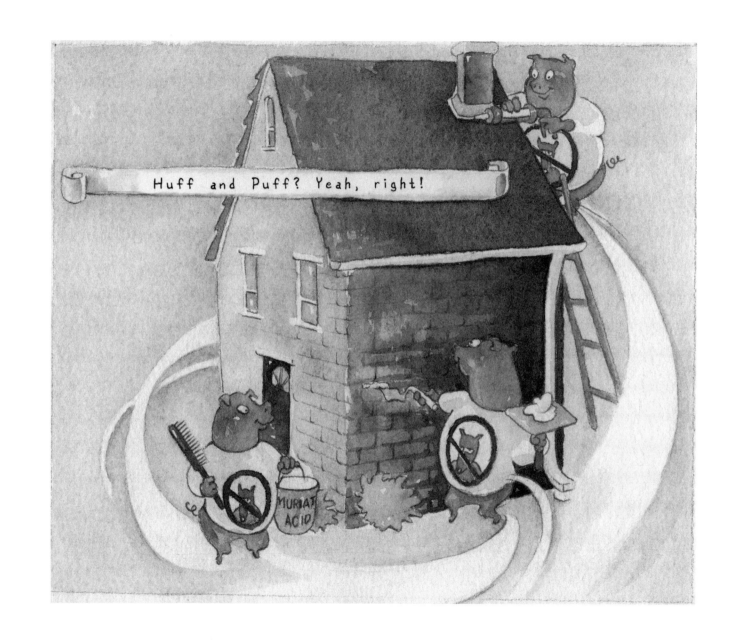

11

OUTER LIMITS

No matter how elite the neighborhood, there's always the inconsiderate twit in the house next door who lets the grass on the front lawn grow high enough to hide a giraffe and then tries to pass it off as a Serengeti wildflower meadow. Sometimes you can reason with such people, but most of us hesitate to explore just how reasonable folks may be. You don't know what kind of pathologies lurk behind a pair of eyes. That's why people creep out in the dead of night to secretly scrawl "wash me" in the dirt buildup on their neighbor's car. That's why anonymous notes were invented. Of course, most of us would never do such things, although the thought crosses our mind in these situations.

The house next door to me had become an eyesore outside. It had been vacant for nearly a year and the absentee owner couldn't find anyone to BUY, RENT, or BARTER for the place, as the obnoxious cardboard sign on the porch pleaded. Advertising circulars piled up on the porch, the grass grew tall, and when the wind kicked up, the trash over there became my trash. I could have continued to call and write and complain to public officials and the owner's nonresponsive agent, but no one was as concerned about the problem as I was—they didn't live next door to it.

Concern about my vested interest in my house is what caused me to swallow my pride, and one of the hardest things about home ownership is swallowing one's pride. Vested interest is not just about individuals and the individual home on which they are paying the mortgage but rather an aggregate of what each homeowner does or does not do in the neighborhood. The value of a homeowner's vested interest plummets over time when neighbors let trash blow because picking it up "is not my job." Vested interest rises when neighbors retrieve blowing trash even when it is on the lawn next door. It may even mean cutting overgrown grass on the lawn of an empty house, as I did, with the only compensation being aesthetic relief.

Of course I would have taken a different tactic had the house been occupied. I still would have picked up the litter, but I would have suppressed my annoyance and offered in a nice genial tone to cut the grass "since I have my mower out." That approach simultaneously offers a helping hand and seeks permission. In other words, sucks up. Maybe the strategy would have softened the relationship and heightened the neighbor's responsibility ethic, or maybe not. I won't know because no one lived there. But I do know that while our homes may be our castles no homeowner is an island.

Naturally, there's more to vested interest than tall grass and an unchecked whirlwind of trash. The care of the exterior facade and surroundings are very important for maintaining the structural integrity of the house. And that job belongs to the folks who live there.

Exterior Walls

Many of us have been conditioned from the cradle that a brick house is the best house. Remember "The Three Little Pigs"? In that tale, the big bad wolf huffed and puffed and blew the straw house down and set fire to the one made of wood. Or maybe it was the other way around. Nonetheless, the only one that withstood the ravages of hot air and arson was the one made of brick. These days, the walls of so-called brick houses still would withstand the felonious assaults of the wolf at the door. But the walls of a brick house are not solid masonry like the third little pig's house presumably was. Solid masonry walls, consisting of several layers of brick or stone or concrete, are most commonly used for garages, retaining walls, garden walls, and commercial buildings. At a residence, a single layer of brick veneer is on the outside, but behind the facade is a framework of wood studs that do the real job of bearing the load. Today's brick house most likely is better insulated than the pig's crib. A lot is going on between the "skin" or exterior of a house and the Sheetrock walls inside. Behind the brick skin is air space, which both enhances insulation and channels any moisture that may have penetrated the exterior walls. Beyond the air space are building paper, plywood sheathing, and wood or metal studs with batts of insulation stuffed between them. The fire was probably the only time the little porker's house was warm.

Stucco homes, like my old baby, are described as brick even though the structure really is three layers of plaster over wood lath. (They skipped the insulation step in my house.) The exterior has lasted for over fifty years with little attention. Stucco homes are like that. However, cracks do develop in the exterior stress points around doors, windows, and chimneys. If not repaired quickly, moisture can seep through and rot the wood framing beneath.

Wood, aluminum, and vinyl are three other types of exterior home siding. They are virtually carefree. Homeowners who want to add aluminum or vinyl siding to the original facade should thoroughly discuss their needs and expectations of the new siding with the contractor before the job is done. If getting better insulation inside the home is the point, siding alone will not do it. Cold air can permeate a three-foot-thick brick wall. The only thing that will minimize the invasion of cold air is a layer of insulation installed between the siding and the original wall. Some home improvement contractors won't mention this since their focus is on selling the aesthetic value of the siding. Insulation is not on their minds. However, it should be on yours.

CARE AND FEEDING OF EXTERIOR WALLS

Wash Me

I know you're not going to do this. Most homeowners don't. I don't have any real enthusiasm for bringing this up. But I feel duty-bound to mention washing the exterior of your house because you should at least know some of the things you should be doing even if you choose not to do them.

Whether the exterior walls are made of brick, stucco, wood, vinyl, or aluminum siding, you should wash them at least once a year. Sometimes a good hosing will do the job, but from time to time you may need to do a little bit more. You might have to scrub. Some stains are stubborn, like **efflorescence.** This is a white powdery crystallization that forms when the water-soluble salts in brick, stone, or mortar are washed to the surface, particularly with new construction. Generally, efflorescence on an older masonry structure indicates there's a leak somewhere. You will have to track it down and fix it.

To clean off the crystallization, scrub on a ten-to-one solution of water and muriatic acid. Muriatic acid is corrosive full strength but is safe to handle in this diluted solution. Use rubber gloves. Pour slowly down the inside wall of the mixing container so that it does not splatter. Also, when adding water pour slowly along the wall of the container. (**Caution:** Muriatic acid should not be stored full strength in just any container. Store the remainder only in the plastic container it came in and keep the container in an out-of-the-way place where it won't be disturbed by human traffic. Under the kitchen sink is *not* a good location. A seldom-used, ventilated portion of the basement or in a garage would be better.)

Wearing rubber gloves, clean small areas at a time with a stiff bristled brush and rinse well.

Mildew is another issue for houses. This fungus is caused by a combination of high humidity and high temperature. You've probably seen it on houses with wood shingle siding. Mildew must be washed away and the surface treated. Painting over it does not remove it. The fungus will only continue to grow through the new coat of paint. A special mildew remover is available at paint stores or mix your own by combining one gallon of warm water to a third of a cup of powdered detergent and a half cup of household bleach. Scrub the entire mildew area vigorously with this solution, then rinse with clean water. Apply one coat of a good grade of undercoat paint and allow it to dry. When the undercoat is thoroughly dry, apply a finish coat of mildew-resistant exterior paint or a top-grade exterior latex paint.

Repointing Bricks and Mortar

Any combination of winter freezing and thawing, excess moisture, and settlement of the house and foundation can cause the mortar around bricks to shrink, crack, and crumble. Brick steps are especially suscepti-ble. These joints are repaired by repointing the bricks—that is, removing the broken pieces and filling, or **tucking,** new mortar into the space with the **point** end of a trowel, hence the expression for the process—tuck-pointing or pointing. Ready-mix mortar is available at building supply stores. Prepare according to directions on the package.

1. Chisel out the old mortar with a cold chisel and hammer to a depth of one-half to three-quarters inch. Be sure to wear goggles.

2. Brush the open joints with a wire brush, then dampen the area, though not to the point of soaking. (The object of dampening the bricks and joints is to prevent the bricks from soaking the moisture out of the mortar mixture.)

3. Using a stiff piece of cardboard to hold the mixed mortar, tuck small amounts of mortar into the spaces using a pointed trowel. Hold the cardboard directly under the area where you are working for ease of application and to catch excess. (The mortar "sets up" or hardens quickly and is difficult to clean up.) Tamp the mortar in place using the flat side of the trowel or a block of wood.

4. When the mortar has hardened just firmly enough for you to leave a thumbprint, smooth it out with a tool called a jointer or use a long piece of metal curved just wide enough to fit along the mortar joint. Pull the metal along the new mortar vertically, then horizon-tally or vice versa.

5. Scrape the edge of the trowel along the area to trim the excess mortar.

6. Once the mortar is set, brush the area with a stiff brush. Dampen the area periodically over three or four days to allow the mortar to cure.

CAULKING

Caulking is used when an airtight or watertight joint is needed where two different materials meet, such as where bathtub and wall tile come together or where the chimney flashing meets the surface of the roof. Caulking's elasticity allows for the natural shifting and movement between joints that occur, for example, when a bathtub is filled and emptied and filled again.

Not all caulking is the same though. There are five basic types of exterior caulking: acrylic latex, vinyl latex, butyl rubber, silicone, and oil-base. Before applying caulking, read the label to see if the surface must be primed first.

Types of Caulk

Acrylic latex: Dries fast. Can be painted. Great for sealing around baseboards and window molding.

Butyl: Bonds well to metal. Good for sealing cracks, joints and around roof flashings, outdoor electrical wall fixtures, and where outdoor faucets protrude from the exterior wall. Water resistant, paintable but messy.

Vinyl: Great for caulking around bathtubs, showers, and sinks. However, paint does not stick too well to it.

Silicone: Long lasting, great around bathtubs, showers, and outdoor uses on masonry, metal, and glass. Does not take to paint.

Oil-base: Inexpensive, dries hard but does not hold up well.

Exterior Painting

It is a big job! There will come a time when your house will have to be painted, but if you're lucky someone else will own it before that happens. It is a time-consuming task that requires plenty of patience, energy, and education about paint and painting conditions. Whether you hire a professional painter or choose to do it yourself, you need to know what is involved both with preparation of the surface and selecting the appropriate paint to use.

Durability and moisture resistance are qualities you want in an exterior paint. Unlike interior paint, exterior paint is made with more resins and pigment, which allow it to withstand rigorous exposure to the elements.

The paint you select depends on the kind of surface to be painted, weather patterns in your area, and where your home is located. If your home is in an area where industrial smoke and fumes are prominent, you will need a paint that is formulated to resist the deposits made by these pollutants. Many of the new paints are designed with a caulking system to be self-cleaning. They gradually chalk and rain washes away the exposed surface dirt. Amazing! Of course, if your house is two-toned with the lower half a darker color than the top, you wouldn't want to use a caulking paint on top, since it will stain anything below it.

Besides the surface to be painted, consider the forecasted weather conditions when the paint job will be done. Painting is a fair-weather task, so wait until there will be a reliable stretch of good weather above forty-five degrees. Temperatures that are too cold or too hot will affect paint performance.

Paints with oil and alkyd bases are very durable once they dry, but they do dry slowly, making the painted surface vulnerable to insects and rain until it is completely dry. Latexes dry quickly but have a tendency to peel if coated over an improperly prepared oil or alkyd-base finish. Paint used on masonry siding must be resistant to the alkali contained in concrete and mortar. The paint's properties generally are printed on the paint can.

Do not hire a professional painter to do the job until you know as much about the task as he/she ought to. The best bet for selecting the appropriate paint is to discuss all of the factors with a reputable paint dealer.

FIXING EXTREME CRACKING OR ALLIGATORING

This happens when a second coat is applied before the first coat dries completely. It also happens when the top coat is incompatible with the underlying coat. Fix the problem by sanding away the problem areas with a power sander. Then brush the area thoroughly to remove dust and loose paint. Apply one coat of a good-quality undercoat paint. Allow the undercoating to dry completely, then apply a top-quality final coat.

REMOVING RUSTY NAIL STAINS

Rust around the nail head is caused by using uncoated steel nails in an area exposed to excessive moisture. Do not simply paint over the stain because the rust will leach through the paint in a short time. Remove built-up rust by sanding or wire brushing the area around and on the nail head itself. Countersink or drive all nail heads until they are just below the wood surface. Apply a coat of primer or undercoat over the cleaned area. Apply caulking compound over the countersunk nail. Let the compound dry and apply one coat of a top-grade exterior paint. After it dries, apply a second coat.

Repairing Stucco

Stucco walls are three layers of cement-based plaster troweled over wood spacers and wire mesh. To fill cracks or repair a large area, add water to a dry-mix mortar. You can add color pigment to the mixture if you wish, although pigment colors are usually limited to pastels.

Chisel out the crack until you reach stucco that is sound. Brush away loose stucco. Dampen the crack and use a putty knife to fill it, packing it in tightly. Cure the patch by wetting it down twice a day for three days.

For a large hole:

1. Chisel out loose stucco back to the mesh and brush away particles. Spray the hole with water.

2. Apply a half-inch-thick coat of stucco using a pointing trowel or putty knife. Push the patch through the mesh wire so that it is embedded with stucco. When stucco is firm but not hard, score the patch area with the point of the trowel or a nail to create horizontal and vertical lines. The stucco will resemble a mesh screen. This first coat is called the scratch coat. Scratching provides a grip for the next layer of stucco. Let the scratch coat sit or cure for at least five

hours. If the house is an open frame wood construction you will have to wait at least forty-eight hours before applying the second coat. In that case keep the first coat moist by misting it twice a day until you are ready for the second coat.

3. Dampen the scratch or first coat and smooth on a second coat to within an eighth of an inch of the surface. Let it cure another forty-eight hours.

4. Dampen the second coat and apply the final coat. Smooth it until it is flush with the surface. Cure for four days.

Repairing and Replacing Aluminum or Vinyl Siding

Sometimes a panel of aluminum siding will sustain an unsightly dent or patch of rust. The panels are fairly easy to repair and replace if making a repair does not solve the problem. Remove rust by rubbing it with fine steel wool. Prime the area with a rust-resistant metal primer and paint with a latex paint.

To repair a bad dent in aluminum siding you will need a drill and a screw to pull the dent out. The screw will serve as a dent puller. Drill a hole in the center of the dent and drive in the screw, leaving enough head exposed to grip with a pair of pliers. Gently pull the screw, pulling out the dent as you go. Back the screw out and fill the hole with plastic aluminum filler. When dry, sand the filler smooth and touch it up with matching paint.

Vinyl and aluminum siding are installed by interlocking each panel. To remove a damaged section of this siding you will need a special tool to separate the interlocked panels. The tool goes by several names. It is best to tell the store clerk what you are trying to do and the proper tool should be recommended.

Clapboard

Typically, these boards split and warp. A damaged board is trouble if not attended to as soon as it is noticed because cracks and splits are entry points for moisture. If left unattended, major damage will occur to the frame and interior wall before any problems are ever noticed externally. The first sign of big trouble is when the paint is peeling from a common wall inside the house. By then, the damage is done.

Repairing a Split Board

Where there is a single horizontal split, carefully separate the damaged board at the split just enough to coat both edges with waterproof glue. Press the glued pieces together and close the crack by driving nails below the lower edge of the board and bending them up. Remove nails when the glue sets.

Grading: Playing the Angles

Everyone knows that water flows downhill. A house at the receiving end of the flow makes a marvelous dam. But that should not be your goal.

Water can be damaging. Having nowhere else to go, the water that has been flowing toward the house eventually comes right on in through hair-line cracks in the foundation and sets right down in the basement. It is important to periodically check the slope of the soil around the house. Soil that is mounded or inclined toward the foundation of the house should be raked and angled away from the house.

WATER the LAWN not the PAVEMent
SHOP FOR USED Tools & Leftover Building MATERIALS
buy BUGS
YE OLDE FLEA MARKET

12

TREE HUGGING 101 AND OTHER ENVIRON-MENTALLY SAVVY STUFF

All of the political jibber-jabber over what is right and what is wrong for the environment leaves many of us not knowing what to think. We are scolded for our environmentally thoughtless habits, which are endangering forests and altering the balance of life in waterways. As a consequence, many of us deal with the debate by tuning it out.

People don't intend to harm the environment. It is just that modern conveniences have put the ecological connection out of sight and consequently out of mind. The conveniences work so well that the complicated functions they simplify are taken for granted. You want light, flip on the switch. You want water, turn a knob. No one's thinking about the turbines and waste treatment plants that bring it all to our fingertips. Few of us living within acres of hard road surfaces ponder the goings-on beneath a concrete sidewalk. So it is unlikely that as a matter of course we would make the connection between habits at home and their effect on the health or decline of waterways and vegetation miles away.

Some of us think storm sewers are connected to waste water treatment plants and that the debris that we throw into the sewer at the curb undergoes a purification process before heading wherever it goes from there. Not so.

The storm sewer's singular purpose is to conduct unpolluted rain and melted snow to the waterways. The storm sewer—not to be confused with the sanitary sewer connected to the waste pipes at home—flows directly into streams, lakes, rivers, bays, and marshes and will deliver to those destinations anything that is thrown into it—antifreeze, gasoline, fertilizers, pesticides, leaves, grass clippings, Styrofoam cups, bottles, dog poo, whatever.

If more of us knew better, we probably wouldn't discard stuff in the storm sewer. This chapter is intended to help us all know better by learning how our routines in and around home impact nature. We will learn what we can do to make ourselves environmentally friendlier.

Water

Up to three-fourths of the earth is water, the same amount, by the way, that there was billions of years ago. But only 1 percent of all this water is usable. That is why waste water treatment plants exist. They clean up and recycle for reuse the water that we use for bathing, cooking, or flushing the toilet.

About 183 gallons of water are treated every day for each person in the United States. The water we drink, cook with, and bathe in is the same water we eventually fish from and swim in. A good treatment plant can do a great job of purifying fouled water, but if the plant is overworked it cannot effectively strip everything that is harmful before sending the water on its way.

For this reason it is important that we think about what we pour down the storm and house drain. A good tour to take would be one to the municipal water system and treatment plants. It will show you how what we do at home can come back to haunt us.

The Lawn

I once was a poor lawn manager. I'm not great now, but I am much better than I was. Before my awakening, I had no system for lawn care except that when the grass grazed my shins I hauled out the mower.

If the mower were easier to access I probably would have cut the grass more frequently. But it had to be dragged up from the basement over uncertain wooden steps and angled through a doorway whose narrow opening was made narrower by an awkwardly hung screen door.

Basement storage was the only way to protect the mower from the free-lancers who prowled the neighborhood every spring, summer, and fall looking for unattended yard equipment they could liberate from beneath the porches where we homeowners stored our stuff for our convenience. What really irritated me about the thefts is that after these felons ripped off your stuff they would boldly show up on your porch some Saturday morning offering to cut your grass. I always declined these offers because I didn't know how I would react if I discovered I was paying a thief to cut my grass with my mower.

Nonetheless, some years my grass looked good and some years it was weedy and terrible. Cutting was all I ever did to it. No seeding, fertilizing, watering, or pampering. Just cutting. I had no clue what I did to make the grass look good or bad or what its basic care was.

One year when the lawn looked really bad I asked one of my neighbors for advice. His lawn was so gorgeous that I am pretty sure he knew what he was talking about, but I lost consciousness listening to him. He seemed mesmerized by lawn ghosts from the past or visions of the future that made him forget I was there as he rambled on. Disappointed, I lumbered back across the street to resume my longing for a lawn that was verdant and inviting.

My neighbor tended his grass like a new lover. He'd weed and feed and clip and edge and pamper that grass from early spring until late fall. During dry, hot spells he'd water it in the early morning and again at night. You'd see him in the dark setting up the sprinklers. He'd spread fertilizers to encourage the grass, spray pesticides to kill the bugs, and spritz herbicides on the weeds and the thatches of grass that pushed up between the cracks in the sidewalk. His grass was prettier and greener than everyone else's. I would not have thought it possible that grass could smile, but I swear on a stack of fertilizer, this gentleman's urban lawn was wearing a big ole country grin.

But like most other green grass fanatics Mr. Gardener's attentiveness was borne more out of aesthetics than environmental concerns. You get a warm and fuzzy feeling coming home to a weed-free, deep green carpet of a lawn, but what does it take to accomplish that look?

Years ago, just about all of the thirty or so families in my neighborhood turned to chemicals to achieve the look. Under the "keeping up with the Joneses" theme, nearly every family independently hired a lawn treatment company to chemically attack the proliferation of weeds out front. The technician would come out and periodically hose down the lawns with whatever it was he was carrying around in that huge tank on the truck. Then he'd stick little yellow flags in the ground printed with a warning to keep off the grass because it had been treated with poison. Even the stray dogs avoided the lawns with the yellow flags. But after a while many of us must have had the same thought about a lawn treatment that required posting hazard signs in front of our homes.

Once applied, these chemicals don't just sit obediently in one spot. They soak into the soil and the groundwater. Any excess is transported through water runoff into storm drains and ultimately into streams, rivers, bays, and waterways large and small that are home to marine life. Not only that, pesticides and other chemicals that are used in abundance threaten human and animal life when they enter aquifers that supply drinking water. It is an absorbing thought.

But an unattended lawn is just as bad as one that is coddled with chemicals. A lawn that is poorly maintained and weedy can lead to soil erosion, surface water runoff, and pest problems. Maintaining a lawn takes forethought, education, and some energy, but pampering is unnecessary.

There are a great variety of grasses. Learning what is what can be puzzling, particularly if you grew up thinking simply that grass is grass. The demystifying process can begin by digging up a few patches of grass and finding out what kind is on the lawn and the type of care it requires.

Take a small patch from different parts of the lawn because a lawn often contains more than one type of grass. Take the samples to a plant nursery or the Cooperative Extension Service in your town. (Every state has one, usually connected with the state university.) They will provide the analytical service and the care advice for free. Just the way you presumably can easily distinguish a rose from a carnation, these experts only have to eyeball the sample to tell you what you have.

Meanwhile, here are some things to think about to develop and maintain a healthy, attractive lawn:

Site Selection

Whether you are establishing a new lawn or want to spruce up the one you have, you should have the grass and soil tested for suitability for its location. For example, there are grasses that grow healthily in shady areas and grasses that don't. The wrong grass in the wrong area can encourage pest and nutritional problems.

Proper Soil Preparation

Do not bury debris on the lawn. Loosen any compacted soil. Grade the soil so that any water runoff is channeled away from the house and onto earth rather than the hard surface of a driveway or sidewalk, for example. Use soil to fill in any holes and depressions in the ground that will collect water. Help the soil and grass by tilling in the recommended proportion and type of lime and fertilizer.

Choosing the Right Grass Species

Unfortunately, there is no pest-free grass. However, there are types of grasses that experience a minimum of pest problems. Find out the best type for your area by consulting a nursery or your state's Cooperative Extension Program. They will probably mention such types as turfgrass, fescues, zoysiagrass, and others. Don't be turned off by the strange language. Just slow the person down and make them speak to you in English until you are comfortable enough with the information to make the selections you need. In addition, many of these places can give you free brochures on lawn care.

Fertilizer

Too much of anything is never good, yet many homeowners believe that the more fertilizer they apply to the lawn, the greener, thicker, more weed resistant it is going to be. Not so. Proper applications of fertilizer can encourage a healthy, dense lawn that recovers quickly from wear, but the applications must be made at the right time of year and in the proportions recommended on the fertilizing product. Inappropriate applications create undesirable lawn conditions such as pests and grass diseases. Too heavy an application also can cause grass to burn and die.

Mowing

Cutting the grass short might reduce the frequency with which you have to cut it, but it can also kill a lawn. All of the grass's food manufacturing is in the blade. Repeatedly cutting the grass too short robs the grass of its source of nutrition and encourages the germination of weed seeds, such as crabgrass and broadleaf weeds, which lie dormant beneath the grass until they are exposed to the sun.

Conversely, grass that is allowed to grow too long or is cut too infrequently can hold too much moisture, which can lead to disease. Some grasses should be mowed to no lower than two inches in height while some can go as low as one and a half inches. That is another reason why it is important to know what kind of grass is on your lawn.

Keep the mower blade sharp and set to a two- to three-inch mowing height. A dull blade will chew up the grass, make it unhealthy, and eventually lead to disease problems.

Controlling Weeds

Weeds compete with the grass and plants for food and water. Although time-consuming, tilling and pulling weeds by hand is the best method of controlling them in small areas. For larger areas herbicides might be necessary. Choose carefully because some of the chemical ingredients in weed killers are harmful to beneficial organisms that live in the ground.

Check with a plant nursery or garden center for the best kind to use. To minimize weed growth between the seams in a concrete sidewalk, grab the weed firmly and pull slowly and steadily to get as much of the root as possible. Scrape any dirt out of the seam and fill it with an expandable latex joint filler.

Grass Clippings

For most homeowners, the most undesirable part of cutting the grass is raking up the clippings. But in most cases you don't have to do that. If you mow regularly and cut no more than the recommended one-third of the blade, you can leave the clippings on the lawn. Decomposed clippings are a natural fertilizer for the soil. Only remove clippings from grass that has been allowed to grow excessively high. Excessively long clippings can smother and rot the grass.

Leaves: Why Rake 'em When You Can Mow 'em

Instead of raking leaves off the lawn in the fall, try mowing them over a few times and leave them as a natural mulch. Mulch mowers have grown in popularity and cost about the same as nonmulch mowers. The advantage of the mulch mower is the blade spins twice as fast as nonmulch mowers, cutting the grass or leaves twice in one movement.

Composting

Why should you? Because it is a practical and convenient way to handle yard wastes. Applications of compost enrich the soil, the flower and vegetable garden, the lawn, trees, and shrubs. It's great for houseplants and other potted plants. Anything that was once alive can be composted.

Nonetheless, there are some organic wastes that are unsuitable for home composting. Avoid morning glory plants, which can be a problem if the seeds are not killed before composting. They will spread. The leaves on buttercups contain an irritating sap and are poisonous. Quack grass is a very invasive perennial grass weed that spreads by seed and a mass of roots that grow horizontally beneath the ground.

Yes	*No*
Flowers	Food scraps
Grass clippings	Diseased plants
Leaves	Weeds with seeds
Old plants	Morning glory plants
Old potting soil	Buttercup
Twigs	Quack grass

WATERING

- Water the lawn only when it needs it. Determine the need by pushing a wood dowel or pencil about six inches into the lawn. If the tip comes up damp, don't water.
- If you feel that you must water, do so but infrequently, deeply, and early in the morning. Allow the lawn to almost get to the drought stage (the grass does not spring back when walked on) and then soak it about three inches using a soaker hose. Watering midday when the sun is strong increases evaporation before the grass has benefited from the moisture. Light, frequent watering at night promotes grass diseases and encourages the shallow growth of roots that are unable to reach the groundwater during droughts.
- Some lawns (bluegrass, red fescue) that begin to brown for lack of

water will go into dormancy. Don't worry and water like mad. Leave it alone. It will naturally recover after the next rainfall.

- Water the lawn, not the pavement. Try soaker hoses. They water the ground slowly, allowing gradual seepage into the soil. Loosen hard, compacted soil to promote air and water circulation in the soil and prevent surface runoff.
- Apply about two inches of mulch to plant beds, including plantings in containers. It will minimize evaporation and the need for watering.

IMPROVE THE DRAINAGE IN YOUR YARD

Water runoff is wasted water. Cities, with their nonabsorbing acres of hard road surfaces, are the main contributors of the runoff that causes flooding and the erosion of topsoil and riverbanks.

Runoff from rainwater and other sources flows into storm drains, creating a torrent that washes away soil. The soft ground, sand, pebbles, rocks, and vegetation that comprise wooded areas are natural breakers for water. They slow the flow, allowing the water to gradually filter through.

At home, rain from the roof and the driveway can erode the soil in a yard and end up in streams and larger bodies of water if not properly channeled. So what? Well, the danger is that the nutrients from fertilizers that you may have added to the soil to improve a garden or lawn contain nitrogen and phosphorous, which, when released into the waterways, produce an excessive growth of algae that robs the water of oxygen and smothers the fish.

PESTICIDES

Use only after exhausting nonchemical alternatives. They don't draw a distinction between beneficial insects and organisms and those deemed harmful. Pesticides can be lethal to both. If you must resort to chemical pesticides read the label and try to avoid those marked WARNING. They are more toxic than the ones marked CAUTION. Buy only the amount you need. Do not exceed the recommended number of applications.

Pesticide Spills

Do not hose down pesticides that have spilled on the driveway, the garage floor, or other outdoor areas. Hosing will carry the chemical to storm sewers and pollute waterways. The best way to clean a small spill is to:

- Sprinkle sawdust, kitty litter, vermiculite, or some other absorbent material over the spill.
- Shovel or sweep the absorbent material into a plastic bag and put it in the trash.
- Wash the area using a solution of water and ammonia or a strong detergent.

PESTS

All lawns contain a diverse community of insects and other organisms that are both harmful and beneficial to plant life. Some insects, such as ants, parasitic wasps, and predaceous beetles, are regarded as beneficial because they are the natural predators of harmful organisms. Maintaining the balance of these adversaries is critical. It is nature's way of providing nonchemical, biological pest control. According to Environmental Protection Agency data there are about 86,000 species of insects in North

America, of which 76,000 are considered harmless or beneficial to humans.

FIGHT BUGS WITH BUGS

Instead of using pesticides you might consider utilizing what the experts call integrated pest management or biological control methods. In other words: Fight bugs with bugs. For example, the praying mantis is the natural predator of the hornworm, which wreaks havoc on tomato crops. The mantis also savors flies.

Ladybugs feast on aphids, aphid larvae, rootworms, and weevils—those little pests that attack a variety of flower and vegetable gardens. You'll develop an appreciation for spiders and the webs they weave when you realize that spiders create these webs to trap their meals, which consist of flies, fleas, treehoppers, and carrot weevils. There are stores that sell beneficial bugs for the purpose of fighting pests without chemicals.

STORM SEWERS

What falls into a storm sewer ends up in our primary waterways. We can help reduce water pollution in storm sewers by doing a few things:

- Maintain a healthy lawn.
- Redirect downspouts from paved areas to vegetated areas.
- Use a rain barrel to catch and store water for gardens.
- Install gravel trenches along driveways or patios to filter water and prevent water runoff.
- Use wooden planks, bricks, or interlocking stones for walkways and patios to slow water runoff.

- Have the driveway and walkways graded so water flows onto lawn areas.

XERISCAPING

This expression comes from the Greek work *xeros* which means "dry." The idea is to maintain a garden that requires as little water as possible by planting a mix of drought-tolerant shrubs, flowers, grass, and ground covers. This, combined with soil irrigation and mulching, will greatly reduce water usage.

NATURAL BARRIERS

Shrubs are a natural for erosion control and for filtering water and air. Planted around a house, shrubs drink from the groundwater, minimizing the opportunity for seepage of moisture through basement walls and floors.

Of course, not all trees are good for planting near a house. Mulberrys, for example, have a very aggressive root system that will barrel through chain link fences and concrete walls. Maples are assertive too. Some trees are bigger drinkers than others. If you have a septic system, a willow can make you weep. However Bradford pear trees, ornamental shade trees, and evergreens are much friendlier. Discuss your tree-planting plans with a nursery before you buy. You might find out that what you like in a tree might not be good for your house.

Born to Shop but Not Retail

What would you say if you could buy a bathroom sink made of faux marble for, say, five bucks, or a five-gallon can of paint for a dollar, or enough fancy carpet squares to cover a twelve-by-twelve room for fifty cents apiece? You'd say what I said: "Yahooey!" There are wonderful places where such treasures can be found. Most of us overlook them because when we think about a tool or fixture we need, it is when we need it, and we want it right away. Consequently, we end up at the home superstore to buy the gadget new.

If we can force ourselves to think "recycle," there are wonderful bargains awaiting us at flea markets and through nonprofit organizations that specialize in recycling building materials at a fraction of the original cost.

The Loading Dock, for example, is a nonprofit building materials recycling center in Baltimore that has soups to nuts in home stuff. The inventory is unpredictable since stock depends on what builders are disposing of at any given time.

However, a conscientious browser who drops in at just the right time can redo an entire bathroom with upscale ceramic fixtures—whirlpool tub, commode, vanitory, shower heads—the works. Usually some percentage of the goods—weatherization materials and paint, for example—are offered free of charge or close to it.

Many of these materials are left over from new construction or renovation projects, and builders having nowhere to store the unused items turn them over to the nonprofit recycling center rather than throw them in a dump, something that has been known to happen to perfectly brand-new goods. Shopping this way not only saves a few dollars but also cuts back on landfill. You may be required to join the service organization for a nominal fee in order to partake.

> ▶ REAL MAN
>
> TIP:
>
> A real man knows how to shop for bargains.

**TREE HUGGING 101
AND OTHER
ENVIRONMENTALLY
SAVVY STUFF**

From time to time these places offer free workshops on cabinet design and installation and other home maintenance and repair needs. Churches, charitable organizations, builders, or the local government may be able to direct you to one near you. If fact, the local government may offer the service itself.

Flea markets, no longer an outlet for unwanted junk, are a source of remarkable finds. You can get anything from a rider mower to basic hand tools and some unique antique tools if you are a collector.

Once upon a time, my motto was "Born to shop." After my exposure to flea markets and recycling centers I changed it to "Born to shop. But not at retail, dahling."

13

CONTRACTORS

So, you've been thinking about making a few improvements around the place. You vividly imagine the conversion of your outdated back porch into an enviable, modern two-level wooden deck with built-in benches and planters. Turning that guest closet on the first floor into a powder room would be practical; or perhaps a bay window in the living room to bring sunlight, curb appeal, and possibly increased property values. Yes, you'll do it!

And then your eyelids begin to quiver uncontrollably. The vision of the finished projects is exciting, but the thought of looking up a home improvement contractor gives you pause. After all, you are a woman—natural prey in the world of renovation and repair. You see the Rip-off Brothers heading your way and you're convinced you will be unable to neutralize them. Ultimately, your enthusiasm takes a hike.

But hold on. It's really not that bad. Yes, 'tis true there are people who call themselves home improvement contractors who have given the industry an enduring warped imaged, but not all are home improvement contractors and not all who are home improvement contractors are disreputable rascals. With that encouraging thought in mind the question becomes:

What Is a Home Improvement Contractor?

For one, 99 percent of them are men. Anyone can call himself a home improvement contractor and many a handyman does. But there are distinctions to be made. By definition, a home improvement contractor (HIC) is licensed. The one who is not is a handyman at best. Not to disparage handymen and handygals. There are some good ones. But there are risks in engaging their services. For one, you give up one of the most important devices a homeowner has—leverage. You may not be able to hold the handyperson responsible if the job goes wrong, even though you may have paid for their services. Their demeanor is great when you're signing them up, but have a dispute involving the money and their attitude—and that of many courts—is they did you a favor so the problem is yours to fix and you may be required to pay whatever balance you may be withholding. Utilizing an HIC ensures a more viable avenue of appeal if things go wrong.

In the narrowest sense, a home improvement contractor improves existing structures, that is, your home. Under this definition, a HIC can turn a closet into a powder room, rebuild the front porch, or change the plumbing system. However, the HIC cannot institute a plumbing system or electrical service in a house where those services did not exist previously, unless he or she holds a license in plumbing and/or electricity.

The HIC usually is licensed in at least one of the trades (electrician, plumber, carpenter) and subcontracts to licensed professionals the tasks he is not licensed to handle.

The benefit of using a licensed contractor is that you at least start out with the law on your side and an overseeing entity to arbitrate any dispute that might arise between you and the contractor. You also presumably have a person who has a maximum amount of training and expertise and who has passed the rigorous licensing examinations for certification in one or more of the trades. A licensed home improvement contractor generally is insured and bonded and subcontracts only to licensed professionals. As such, the HIC is held liable for the shoddy work of the subcontractors. And as with anything else in life, there are good HICs and some not-so-good HICs.

Typically, local governments will require permits for major home renovation jobs. You should check the rules and regulations of your town. I can hear your resistance. When it comes to your place, "An ignorant public official is a happy public official," you say. Maybe. But that attitude can backfire. Embrace this adage: "It's better to be safe than sorry." Example. You rim your house with an eight-foot-high privacy fence, then you discover there's a six-foot rule on the law books for the area your house is in! The expensive fence must come down. That's too much to put out in costs, aggravation, and time.

What's more, filing for a permit alerts you to other important issues you may not have thought of, such as the requirement that you contact your utility company. Electrical, gas, and telephone lines may be located beneath the job site. You wouldn't want to dig and sever a power line. The utility companies need to be advised of the work you plan so they can come out and identify where their lines are before construction begins. They do this by checking their records on your house, then marking the ground with color-coded symbols to indicate the location of the underground utility lines. If you destroy a line, you will be financially responsible for the repair cost.

I'd Rather Do It Myself

Great! You can be your own contractor and do anything in your home yourself. But don't be too prideful to seek help when it's needed. If you are replacing your plumbing system yourself, for example, talk at length with a professional plumber at a hardware store or one of those home improvement centers before you do the job. There are rules, for example, governing lead-based solder, where it can and cannot be used, and other peculiarities of which you may be unaware. Once you've completed the job, have a professional inspect your work. It may cost you a small fee but it will be worth it. After all, you've saved a bundle by doing the job yourself in the first place.

Avoiding Conflicts

Most contractor conflicts are preventable. Often, they grow out of a customer's insecurities, preconceived notions, and misconceptions. That should be an empowering thought. When fault can be traced back to ourselves, so can the solutions and preemptive measures.

For example, there could be a misunderstanding on your part about what the contractor is obligated to do. Don't guess or leave things to chance. Ask questions and write the answers down. Too often we think we shouldn't "bother" them with our questions. Bother them! Unfamiliarity with the home improvement culture leaves us too suspicious and ill informed for our own good. Before making that first call to a potential

CONTRACTORS

contractor, do yourself a favor and conduct groundwork. It is a lesson I learned the hard way and I gladly share with you the story and the solutions as a cautionary tale.

Once upon a time, I hired a contractor to install a privacy fence around my backyard. On the first day, a half dozen workers arrived at my home as scheduled, gung ho and hauling a ton of lumber, bags of cement, an impressive array of tools—all of which they dumped in the driveway. I was forced to park at the curb. That was inconvenient but a mere trifle considering that in just a couple of days I was going to have a stunning new fence in plenty of time to show off to my relatives who were coming for a Fourth of July backyard picnic that was three weeks away.

Working like beavers, the crew took down the old chain link fence and dug holes all around the yard for the posts for the new fence. With the old fence gone and the new one not yet up I felt naked and vulnerable. The open yard was a bald invitation to the neighborhood pests who thrived on liberating other folks' belongings. But I made provisions. Along with some other stuff I didn't want to lose to the liberators, I wheeled the lawn mower around to the front of the house, dragged it up the steps, and secured everything in the kitchen.

At day's end, the work crew packed up their small tools and said, "See ya tomorrow bright and early." It's the last I saw of them for several days. Why? Who really knows? The reason the contractor gave for each day that no crew showed up was as original as "The dog ate my homework." On Day 1 it was "The truck broke down." The next day the same truck was in an alleged accident. A nationwide company with only one truck! Day 3, the excuse was the occupants in the "accident" truck sustained—wouldn't you know it—back injuries. Day 4 the explanation was illness, which felled the foreman, a fellow whom I noticed was so blatantly youthful that not a trace of hair was evident on his chest and face. I guessed that he was ill all right. He probably came down with a case of chicken when he realized the job he was supposed to be supervising was way over his head. Contractors don't necessarily hire workmen who prove in advance that they know how to do the job. Many workers are relatives and the sons of relatives who are hired merely as seven-dollar-an-hour muscle, and for a lot of them, the task at your house is weekend date money. And for still others, it's on-the-job training.

By Day 5 the contractor obviously had run out of excuses because it was one o'clock in the afternoon and I had neither seen nor heard from the work crew. It was left to me to track down somebody at the company who might have an idea of when a work crew might be back at my place to continue the job. Now, see, you thought stuff like that only happened to you. Doesn't it feel good knowing your misery has company.

There was a little quirk in the work of contractors I should have known about at the time but, like marriage, I really could not have discovered it until after the fact. That first day of bustling activity has a name and a purpose. It is a tactic called "sealing it in," or what I call "gotcha." It is intended to do exactly what it did: gain my confidence and lock me in.

I discovered that while we customers might be concerned about getting the job *done*, contractors are concerned about getting the job *started*. With the contract begun and "sealed in," the contractor can go off on Day 2, 3, 4, etc. and start other jobs when he should be at your place building a fence. I was angry enough to cancel the project, but with a yard full of holes and a driveway blocked with building materials it wasn't likely. And the contractor knew this all too well. Hence, gotcha.

WHAT TO DO?

I thought about giving him a piece of my mind. But all that would have done was give me a phony sense of power and make him predictably surly and stubborn. The situation called for wile. Since this was a high-profile

217

CONTRACTORS

business, I called the library to research the name of the company's president. Having found out who it was, I telephoned him and told him my problem. He appeared sympathetic to the situation and promised immediate action.

However, the immediate action dragged by another two days with no work crew. It was becoming obvious that the work would not be finished on time. I put my complaint in writing, stating in the very first paragraph the exact remedy I wanted. Subsequent paragraphs filled in the background of the problem. The letter was short and to the point, calm but firm, assertive yet nonthreatening, urgent yet not desperate. I faxed the missive to the top guy, with a copy to the project manager who had signed me up for the sale in the first place.

The project manager called later that day apologetic and full of more promises. I suppressed my cynicism. Apparently, it paid off. The next morning, a crew appeared and worked the job until it was completed three days later. The day before the finish, the project manager came out to inspect the progress. He thanked me for my patience and told me he appreciated my pleasant demeanor under the circumstances and asked if there was anything he could do to make up for the inconvenience.

It was the finest act of contrition I had heard from a contractor. It was worth the forks I bent in half trying to control my temper. There was a gate I neglected to include in the original contract, so I chose as my consolation prize a gate at the back end of the yard to replace the decrepit one I had rigged up a few years earlier. He agreed to build a new gate. The moral of the story is you can get more with honey than with vinegar. And applying honey in a situation does not mean the user is a sap.

I could have yielded to my anger and gotten nasty on the telephone, made empty threats, complained to my state's Home Improvement Licensing Board, the Better Business Bureau, or some other authority right away. But that would have ticked off the contractor and I wouldn't have seen that fence that year or any other. Or I could have threatened the contractor with canceling the job. But then we would have wasted time in an acrimonious haggle over how much I owed him for the day the crew dug holes all over the yard. I still would have had to pay someone else to finish what was started. I kept my mind focused on *my* bottom line: Get the fence. Get it before the Fourth of July. Get it this year. Accomplishing that goal required dogged diplomacy and a strategem.

As a rule, women tend to be more diplomatic than men, and that approach often is mistaken for weakness. But it is an approach that is critical in home repair negotiations. Diplomacy can work for men as well. It keeps tempers cooled. Be pleasant but consciously firm about what you want. Contractors don't respond well to threats or Scarlett O'Hara tirades. But they are responsive to a nonwaffler who can state exactly what she wants and do so in a way that pricks the conscience and sense of reason.

Of course, no contractor is going to come right out and admit to the "sealing it in" practice. And it would be counterproductive to fling that knowledge in his face. But it is important that *you* know it exists and to be prepared. Forewarned is forearmed.

Why You Should Ask "Why?" and "Why?" Again

Asking questions is good. Very young children do this. They not only ask trenchant questions—"Why is the sky blue?"—but they've got great follow-up—more "whys?" As we grow into our teens we ask fewer questions. Hell, we know it all then. Into adulthood the queries drop off even further. We aren't necessarily wiser. We know we don't know everything but we're embarrassed about that and don't want to ask questions and betray our ignorance. Heaven forfend. Even when we get around to asking a few questions, we don't process the answers as if merely asking was enough. There is a point to all of this, really.

I moved from a five-bedroom house into a two-bedroom condominium. My goal was to better utilize the new space, which was smaller than I was accustomed to. The task was to establish plumbing and electrical lines in a large closet to create a compact laundry room with a full-sized washer and dryer. Mr. Contractor said that because of the plumbing that would be added to the area, the closet doors needed four more inches of clearance in order to close. His solution was to construct a new doorframe, building it out by four inches, reattach the doors, and finish off the look with fancy floor-to-ceiling Greek columns or some darn thing to make the alteration look natural. My initial response was, "Cool. You're the expert." But the more I thought about the plan the more I asked myself, "Why? Why? Why?"

According to my measurements of the area and the appliance there was tight but adequate space, even with plumbing, with no need for added construction. I needed to ask a few questions. I knew that walls generally have at least four inches of play behind them. "Why couldn't the machines be recessed four inches instead of building out the doorframe?" I asked.

"The main drain runs at an angle in the wall and would be in the way," Mr. Contractor said. "Okay, why not recess just the plumbing for the washer? Or why not mount the hot and cold water pipes onto the wall to one side of the washer instead of directly behind it, thus allowing the machine to slide back and clear the doorframe. Finally, I had hit a "why" to which Mr. Contractor had no rejoinder.

"We could do that," he said.

"Well, why didn't you think of it?" I asked.

He chuckled. It was the kind of nervous snicker fathers make when their daughters have effortlessly and obviously outthought them in their own territory with simple logic. I didn't think it was so funny. I had allowed my faith in my own ability to think to take a backseat to Mr. Contractor's alleged expertise.

Stay alert. It is all right to give supposed experts the benefit of the doubt, but only after you have thought the problem out yourself. I nearly let a few unasked "whys" come between me and the several hundred dollars Mr. Contractor consequently shaved off the bill for the modified contract. Remember that contractors are salesmen and the product they are selling is their service. Be a critical consumer.

Finding a Contractor

TEN PRECAUTIONS

1. Avoid the ones who call or show up unsolicited at your door, even when they seem nice and helpful. The "I'm doing work in your neighborhood . . . " line is almost never true. Be the hunter, not the hunted.

2. Deal only with licensed professionals. Get their home improvement license number and confirm it with the licensing board.

3. Licensed or not, avoid those contractors who have only a post office box number and no street address, or whose telephone number produces only an answer machine.

4. Do not pay cash.

5. Never pay more than one-third of the total contract in advance.

6. Give up no money until you have in hand a written contract signed by both parties.

7. Don't pay for estimates. The only acceptable estimate is the "free" estimate.

8. Don't rush. Shop around. Get estimates from several contractors before deciding. Don't let their promise of a "discount for deciding today" hustle you into an impetuous decision.

9. Get references and check them! Make specific inquiries about the contractor's timeliness and the quality of his work. Call your Better Business Bureau or Consumer Protection Agency to see if there is a complaint history for the particular contractor.

10. Cost is important, but don't let that be the sole reason for the contractor choice you make.

Getting an Estimate

TEN QUESTIONS TO ASK

1. **What? Why? How come?** Be as unabashedly inquisitive as a five-year-old. The answers will help you decide what estimate is reasonable. Take written notes; rely on them rather than what you think you remember.

2. **How much?** Get a breakdown of the total estimate. How much is for materials and how much is for labor.

3. **What's included?** Do not expect that the electrical contractor, for example, will install a fixture in the laundry room where you've hired him to run electrical lines if that is not explicit in the contract. In his mind that is two jobs. Does the $10,000 estimate for

the new kitchen include the refrigerator, the dishwasher, the sink, and faucet of your choice?

4. **What quality materials?** Can you substitute higher-cost materials for lower-cost without sacrificing long-term efficiency or quality? To better judge the contractor's response, find out ahead of time what materials are involved and comparison shop.

5. **How long?** The contractor says the job will take five days. Find out about those five days; they may not be consecutive. Will the contractor make a commitment to stay with the job every day until it is completed? Get a begin date and a target end date written into the contract. Determine an agreeable end date by adding on a minimum of ten float days to whatever date the contractor says he or she will finish the job. Building in flexibility is good public relations on your part and sets the right tone from the start.

6. **Interruptions?** What situations are likely to delay the work. Don't accept the old "unforeseen circumstances" line on its face. Get a few "for instances." If the job is outside, weather delays are a legitimate consideration. An inside job might entail unexpected structural problems. Discuss the possibilities in detail. You might not hit all the permutations, but you will have an idea of the things that can cause a delay.

7. **How many workers?** When comparing contractors' labor charges it is important to know how many people, including subcontractors, will work the job. A large company may require only two days to do a job with five workers. A small company may charge the same amount but take ten days to complete the job using only two workers.

8. **How will I be charged?** Find out if you will be charged by the job or by the day. The estimate generally is based on the amount of time it typically takes to do the job. By the job, you pay a fixed cost, no matter how long it takes. Paying by the day, you pay for the number of days it takes to complete the work. However, a job can drag on, and you'll have to pay for each day required to complete it, thus transferring cost control from your hands into those of you-know-who.

9. **Don't start a rush job.** Practicality says the job will take ten business days, you need it done in eight, the contractor says it can be done in five. Don't fall victim to ego and desire. Stick with practicality and postpone the nonemergency job until time permits.

10. **Who hauls the trash?** There may be a considerable amount of trash from the job, particularly with remodeling. Find out who will be responsible for hauling the trash away. In short, put an assuming tone in your questions so that you get real answers. "Have you ever beaten your wife?" will get you a predictable denial. "When did you stop beating your wife?" will bring at least a stutter if not the truth.

The Contract

1. Don't sign until you have explored all of your options.

2. In some states you have a few days after signing to cancel without a penalty. Check out your state's regulations regarding contractors.

3. Have someone you trust and who has a sharp eye read the contract before your sign. Look out for "second mortgage" and "assignment"

language. They are red flags for trouble. Pay by credit card when possible. That way you have a good record and you stand a better chance of halting payment if that becomes necessary.

4. Any agreement should include:

- Description of the work to be done
- Materials to be used
- Materials' cost
- Labor cost
- Names of subcontractors
- Timetable, including completion date
- Payment schedule and financing arrangements
- Warranty agreements
- Cleanup responsibility

5. Don't pay the balance until you are completely satisfied.

On the Job

NO-NO'S

1. Do not try to make the workers feel at home. They are not. Let them provide their own lunch and beverage, although you can make cold water available through an outside spigot or jug.

2. Don't fraternize with the help.

3. Don't ask about the spouse and kids. You're the site supervisor. Your only concern is the job at hand.

4. Don't provide health aids. Let 'em bring their own tissues.

5. Don't harass the workers or criticize the job they are doing.

6. Limit your complaints and discussions to the foreman.

7. Be inquisitive but don't nag.

8. Treat the workers respectfully.

9. Do not settle for an unsatisfying answer.

10. Don't leave it all up to the contractor. Reputable home improvement companies appreciate cooperative customers who work with them to complete the project.

Top Ten Stupid Contractor Tricks

1. Says your husband has to be home in order to have home improvements discussion with you.

2. Pulls out pictures of the offspring.

3. Tells a tender story about the little cherub's dance recital.

4. Shows up uninvited on your doorstep and says he's doing work in your neighborhood.

5. Calls you in the middle of your supper so you agree to an appointment just to get him off the telephone.

6. Tries to get you to replace the entire roof when repair of a small damaged portion is all that's needed.

7. Says the roofing bill covers fixing the rotting soffit and overhang and because you're a nice lady he will reseat the gutters for free.

This is no favor. He'll have to remove the gutters to do the repair work anyway. Replacing them is a part of the job.

8. Tells you he noticed that all of your windows are rotting and should be "replaced before the cold weather sets in. And I hear this winter's going to be real bad."

9. Starts demolition so you can't change your mind but once started doesn't show up for a few days.

10. Buys a cheap grade of commercial paint but charges you for premium.

True Lies

Some people can look right in your eyes and with a straight face present as fact fiction they are inventing right on the spot. I found that the phenomenon occurs a lot between contractor men and the women who hire them. Sometimes the lies are surprisingly bold.

Take the dishwasher incident. I hired a contractor to, among other things, relocate my dishwasher from my old house to my new place. He is licensed as a home improvement professional and had proved to be skilled and reliable in the past. He set about connecting the machine in its new spot. From where I was standing it looked like one side of the machine's metal frame was bent, curved inward at the bottom as if it had been transported with all of its weight leaning on one side.

"The frame's bent," I said. The professional license stepped back to get a better look and without missing a beat said: "Oh, the frame's designed that way so the machine can fit into any cabinet space." My mind skipped a few frames in disbelief. I searched his face for the cue that he was, perhaps, joking? He was serious. This particular day I didn't have the stomach for confrontation, so I decided against telling him I knew he was making stuff up. Instead, I humored him like mothers humor three-year-olds into picking up their toys.

"You know," I said, "the floor's crooked, sort of sloped. Why don't we bend the frame so the machine is even with the floor. The frame will look straight, even though it is not supposed to be, but that would solve the problem of the door grating against the springs every time I open it. What do you think?" I asked plaintively. "That just might work," he said, giving me an officious nod of approval. "Let's try it," he added. We did and, of course, with the frame now "straightened" the machine fit into the space just fine.

Another of my favorite all-time contractor falsehoods is the "Your husband has to be home" routine. The whole scenario usually begins just as you've sat down to supper. The telephone rings and it's a deal on replacement windows. The timing of the call is intentional: Catch people while their tongue is drooling and they'll agree to anything to get back to their meal. So you agree to a free estimate and set a date. Then *the* question: "Will Mr. Homemaker be home at that time?"

"No, he won't."

"Well, why don't we set up a time when he's there?"

"That's all right, you can talk to me."

"No, we need to talk to your husband."

"Why?"

"Because it's the law."

"Oh?!"

When I insisted on knowing more about this law, the caller hung up on me. The law he was talking about does not exist except in the "Salesman's Solicitation Rule Book." It's called the spousal leverage rule. It works when the salesman can play one spouse against the other. Mr. Spouse says "No," so Mr. Salesman makes eye contact with Mrs. Spouse, prompting her to launch an appeal in that voice Mr. Spouse cannot resist until Mr. Spouse cries uncle. Mr. Salesman then follows up with the "How can you deny the little lady her heart's desire, you beast," tone.

However, if Mrs. Spouse is the holdout, Mr. Salesman leans on Mr. Spouse's ego with the "I know *you* wear the pants in this house" challenge. The idea is to ego wrestle that male pride into signing on the dotted line.

The scenarios may sound sickeningly stereotypical, but contractors use this psychology because it is proven to work. With only one person to deal with, the contractor has to work harder, with the results less predictable. Stay alert. Question the logic. Get what *you* want.

Next to single women, the salesman's next favorite targets are widows, widowers, and senior citizens.

SENIOR CITIZEN SCAMS

After many decades of activity and acuity, many senior citizens let their guard down. The maintenance and repair around the house go unattended such that it is noticeable to passersby. These are the signs that unscrupulous contractors actually drive around looking for. They play on fears and prey on elderly folks who may not be as skeptical as they once were. The elderly homeowner enters into a repair agreement without checking with anyone and is surprised to find a final bill of costs they didn't think they agreed to. The contractor insists on payment, which he had figured all along the homeowner did not have.

He files a mechanic's lien against the property and in many instances can force a sale of the house to recover whatever money he claims is due. It is a dastardly thing to do to a person, but unfortunately not all vultures have wings.

Sometimes we'd rather stay to ourselves but we should make a special effort to look out for elderly neighbors. They often need help and many are too stubborn and cautious to ask for it.

Think Ahead

It's summer and you're having a hall closet converted into a powder room. Remember insulation before the walls go up! You'll thank yourself in the winter.

For a stamped preaddressed envelope, many state and consumer protection groups will send you free publications with tips on how to work with contractors.

14

A "REAL MAN"

The Profile

Every now and then my gal pals and I get together and talk about men. Surprise! Two margaritas and we're reeling off withering one-liners, laughing until our sides ache. Inevitably, someone brings up the touchy subject of the black hole.

You know the black hole—that hypothetical collapsed star out in space with the intense gravitational pull. My pals believe there is nothing hypothetical about that hole or its pull. It has had serious consequences on earth, having sucked the planet's supply of "real men" out into its void.

We know the "Real Man" (*ReMa*—pronounced "ree ma") once roamed the earth in force in the post-troglodyte era and was highly visible in the last three centuries. We read about the species as little girls, saw him in docudramas; they were men with an edge: Sir Lancelot, Robin Hood, Tarzan, the Lone Ranger, Shaft, Superfly, Rocky. One of his main characteristics was his ability to listen, to hear a woman's voice and think what it was saying was important. He was intuitive, could make good conversation, and make a great omelette as well.

Grown up, we gals were unable to quiet the longing for the ReMa man of our adolescent imagination. We looked but they seemed impossible to find. Every now and again we thought we found one. Alas, too often, closer inspection revealed not a genuine ReMa but a ReMa decoy. To soothe our disappointment we got together for periodic wakes where we'd drink margaritas and emit a mournful query from deep within: "Where are they?" But before that question can be answered one must explore this one: "What are they?"

The "Encyclopedia of Real Men" that my friends and I rely on describes a real man as ruggedly handsome, muscled, sensitive, sartorially aware, a witty stud. To qualify he must possess at least three of the qualities, with "sensitive" a must feature and an added essential requirement that he can fix stuff.

A male friend to whom I revealed this description in the hopes of getting some ReMa location tips suggested that women are looking in the wrong places. He said the men we are trying to find are primarily in Orlando, Florida, at Walt Disney World. What women want in a man, he claims, is a fantasy. To that I say, "Ya darn tootin'!"

A woman can do wonders with a fantasy. She can conjure up imaginary playmates and work them until they are real. It is a skill daughters learn from their mothers. "If you can conceive it you can achieve it." Of course, you must be careful what you wish for.

My guy friend was right on one point: Women have been looking in the wrong places for that real man. Happy-hour bars are not good ReMa locators. Bars field a predictably disappointing crop of twits in three-piece suits who are unlikely to take on any activity that could risk chipping a professional manicure, and it is themselves they talk about endlessly.

Barbecues and crab feasts produce the married guys with their families, and married guys—many of whom are ReMas—belong with their married wives who discovered them. An outing at art museums generally dissolves into yawners when the exhibits you really want to see seldom cross the gallery threshold. However, despite this sad picture, there have been genuine ReMa sightings.

So let's cut to the chase. The best location to look for a ReMa in the nineties is in the home project centers. These oversized hardware stores are a fun house of bulging biceps, a Jurassic Park of real men. ReMa potentials pour through those portals in a feverish swell. Sure, sometimes they are wearing sweaty T-shirts. But a gal can get used to salt stains if the guy in the T-shirt can hold a conversation and he can fix stuff.

Of course, not all men who come through these places are ReMa. In fact, there are ReMa look-alikes who possess one or two of the basic qualities that get your attention, but closer inspection reveals they are decoys. It is equally important to know how to spot a ReMa as it is to recognize a ReMa decoy, so let's examine the fakes first.

The Decoy: "That Fish Was How Big?"

If you've ever witnessed a conversation about sports, you know this profile. Sports is a big topic for both the ReMa and the ReMa decoy.

The decoy will recite, for example, baseball statistics on players no one has thought about since World War I. Plenty of times he's giving bogus information. But who's going to question whether Enos Slaughter really stole more bases than Ricky Henderson? Most women don't care about that particular tiny print and therefore are the decoy's favorite audience. In an effort to impress, the decoy fakes facts, often with impunity.

On the other hand, a ReMa will freely admit to what he does not know, and if he thinks the information is important enough to anyone he will look it up and have solid information the next time they meet.

When it comes to women, the decoy feels obliged to let a woman know that he knows something that she doesn't, no matter how obscure, how irrelevant.

Take the decoy in aisle B7 of the home project center. I needed to patch a hole in a plaster wall. I knew how to do it. I'd done it before. I was in a rush, unfamiliar with the layout of the warehouse, and just needed to know where to find the joint compound quickly.

"What's it for?" B7 asked.

"To patch a hole in a wall."

"What kind of wall?"

"Sheetrock."

"Doing the job yourself?" he asked with an approving smile.

"Yes," I said, anxious to find the stuff and get out of there.

"With EZ Does It compound you'll be done in an hour," he advised, pitching an off-brand in that deep-throated voice of authority men put on when they want to be believed.

"All's you have to do is slap it on and paint right over it."

Well, I knew that wasn't true. You need at least two coats of compound, and each coat has to dry between applications. Then you have to sand the area and prime it before painting. He was wrong. We both knew it, but we just played each other along. Intrigued by his bold ability to unflinchingly dispense untruths, I asked questions. He got deeper into his fabrications and I egged him on with more questions. It was amusing, but I knew he was no ReMa.

Studies have shown that it is a combination of the hormone testosterone and the way society conditions its boys from the cradle to protect their female counterparts that makes them tell whoppers.

The rehearsal starts when they are youngsters playing macho development games, rescuing the princess from the evil dragon. They grow up with an acute case of "Knights in Shining Armor Syndrome," a condition activated by questions posed by females.

These knights instinctively do whatever is necessary to prevent getting caught with their knowledge down around their ankles. The studies have found that the psyche and biology of these poor fellows eventually operate in conflict: Machismo makes them want to help the damsel in distress but testosterone makes them lie.

Discovering ReMa

As in any shopping mall, you don't want to go in without a strategy. Project centers have so much stuff, a trip there can be distracting if you don't have a plan. One can lose one's sense of purpose and make selection errors. We already know that not every man is a ReMa, but when they are on the shelf, as it were, side by side like so many brands of canned tomatoes, it's easy to reach for the wrong one. Shopping for a ReMa requires basic logic for starters.

For example, when you go to the supermarket for lamb chops, you don't just go to the meat case, you specifically go to the section where the lamb is. For chicken you go to the poultry counter. For cookies you go down the cookie aisle, and so on. ReMa shopping at home project centers isn't too much different.

ReMas can be found in several aisles. If noticeable biceps, triceps, and deltoids are important features to you, check out the building materials department. This is where they are. Watch for the guy who picks up two five-gallon buckets of, let's say, joint compound or roofing tar—one in each hand (that's 61.7 pounds each!)—and carries them off without a cart.

▶ **REAL MAN
TIP:**

The difference between
men and women is not
only the plumbing, it's in
the wiring too.

The mesmerizing sight of this will have you following him to check him out in the checkout line. But wait! Think about this: Did he carry those buckets with ease all the way to the front of the store or did he struggle even though he passed empty shopping carts all along the way that he could have used. He may be a strong man, but he's not a thinking woman's kind of strong man. A ReMa gets help when help is needed.

You want a brainy, stoic ReMa? Welcome to the electrical department. No notable biceps here, but the subjects who travel these aisles are calm though electrifying thinkers, ReMa potentials who can spark your interest. These fellows respect power, know how to use it, and welcome a little challenge to their circuitry.

Your sensitive ReMas can be found in the garden centers that many of these stores developed a few years ago to attract female consumers. It was a good strategy. These ReMas can easily be overlooked, since they tend to wear shirtsleeves. Quiz him. If he knows the plants by their botanical names he's more than likely a ReMa.

Still, shopping in stores is not for everyone. If you find the home project centers a bit more than you can take, you can always shop at home. Whenever I needed repair work that I could not do myself cost-effectively, I put the job out for bid. (By the way, nothing has to be broken to have it fixed.) Schedule the interview of potential handymen for different days. I used to set up same-day morning and afternoon appointments. But you can run into trouble if the morning guy is late and shows up at the same time as the afternoon appointment.

Never take the first bid offered, even if it sounds reasonable. That way you get to see more. As each of these handymen parade in to look over the job, you can look over him. It's like shopping at home from an interactive catalog with moving pictures.

Obviously, this approach is presented to you with tongue planted firmly in cheek. Nonetheless, I discovered that a whole new galaxy appears for the woman who takes charge of her house and gets to know what's involved in its workings, repairs, and maintenance. It is a wonderful way to meet interesting people whose paths you otherwise might never cross. The bonus is you learn an exclusive language that is equivalent to learning the secret handshake of a boys club.

The astrological black hole may be a real phenomenon, but it is nice to know there are "real men" escaping its gravitational pull. They can be found at a hardware store, where many of them confess to going to find "real women." But that's another story.

15

ETCETERA

The Junk Drawer

There is so much left I want to share with you but none of it fit very neatly in previous sections. So rather than leave these little nuggets out, I thought I would create the book version of a junk drawer.

Every living space has one somewhere, even if it is just a box. We all know that the junk drawer doesn't really contain junk. We know junk when we see it, and that gets tossed pretty fast. It's the odds and ends that had a limited purpose once, are still functional, and one day may come in handy, but for now . . .

This drawer usually contains small stuff you got tired of sorting and thus unceremoniously swept out of sight. The junk drawer usually is in the kitchen. It sometimes goes unopened for weeks, even months, until you have a need for the miniature hole puncher you had a vague idea you might find somewhere in there.

The beauty of the drawer is its eclecticism.

Anything could be in there. The mix is both of the useful and momentarily useless variety, a collection of "one-day" things that you figured you might need one day but probably wouldn't learn what for until the day after you threw it out.

So you save the rubber bands from the daily paper, lengths of string, tubes of glue, the screwdriver with the broken handle, pliers, nuts and bolts, the extra soy sauce and catsup packets from the takeouts, the "Junk Drawer Organizing" sheet with the lift-off labels that have never been lifted off, the collection of yellow trash bag ties, the broken pot handle, a recipe for gingersnaps you copied from a TV cooking show but never used, buttons, triple-A batteries, an assortment of keys—including one for a pair of old Union-brand roller skates you haven't owned in a dog's age—flasher bulbs for the Christmas tree lights, a shoe horn, matchbooks, scissors, two dozen receipts for items you meant to return a few years ago, and $14,750 in Monopoly money.

But it is okay. Whether they are organized or confused, junk drawers are okay. They hold confusion that otherwise could be in our heads.

The Tomorrow Room

For the stuff too big to fit in the junk drawer, there's the tomorrow room. Some homes have more than one tomorrow room—one in the attic and another in the basement, perhaps. After three uses we realize that the Belgian waffle iron we just had to have wasn't really "all that," after all. We could sell it off or give it away, but we have to wait until the guilt-ridden sense of money wasted wears off. So we gradually push it to the back of a cabinet and eventually take it to the attic or basement, where just before we slam the door shut we vow, "I'll get to it tomorrow."

I learned how bad that habit was when I moved from a single-family home to an apartment. There was no tomorrow room. There was hardly enough space for today. When I asked for the key to the storage area, a potential tomorrow room, I thought, the building manager said, "Here you go—your bin is in the storage room on the third floor." As I made my way there I kept wondering: "Why'd she say bin?"

Inside, the storage room looked like a huge chicken coop with yards of chicken wire stapled over one-by-twos forming elongated cubicles with ten-foot-high ceilings. You could measure each bin with a twelve-inch ruler. Each had its own chicken-wire door with a combination lock on it. It was a "stuff" prison. I couldn't let my stuff end up like this. I vowed that day that whatever I keep for tomorrow I'm going to make sure I can use it today.

Sleep It Off

We've all had one of those days where it feels like we are the straight woman in somebody's stand-up routine. Nothing planned goes right and the unexpected goes wrong. A friend says those are the days when the devil has crossed his legs. Yeah, made me pause too. But the imagery is irresistible: Beelzebub posing in a fireproof chair, elbow on the table, a flinty hand stroking his Vandyke, legs crossed and cloven hoof dangling back and forth. His lips are moving and he's saying "Have a nice day." And then the fun begins.

This particular day, I had plenty to do. Each activity tenuously hinged on the perfect execution of the other. The morning began real early. First the basement. The dampness on the basement floor that I had attributed to a high water table from the last rains was not drying up but building up. It turned out that the source was the water heater.

I should have gotten my first hint from the morning showers that cooled down quicker than usual. I started to call the utility company, but only two months earlier I had dropped the service contract I had maintained on the hot water heater for twelve years. It figures. I thought I could save money, since I never had any problems in all the years I maintained the contract. But now I needed it but didn't have it.

Do I patch or replace? My decision making was interrupted by the sound of a diesel engine plowing through my block at top speed. That's how witnesses have described tornadoes. One was twisting its way through my block. But hey, why not? It rearranged the porch furniture and had its way with the welcome mat and the faux wood shutters on the windows. Blew them to pieces. Then the power went out. I couldn't call anyone because the only telephone I had was a portable that required electricity. Some days, there's only one sensible thing to do when the devil decides to cross his legs. Take a nap. After a few hours sleep, decisions are far easier to make.

Delegate, Delegate, Delegate

Women are the mules of society. It is not a very glamorous image but it's true. Even in this age of high feminist awareness, society still conditions its female members from the cradle to be chief cook, bottle washer, wet nurse, and all-around nurture-provider. The conditioning is so thorough that women perform these roles with one foot on the corporate ladder reaching for success and trying not to bump her head on the ceiling and the other foot on the kitchen step stool reaching for the Cocoa Pops.

Youth makes you think you can do it all, and many a young gal sets her hair on fire trying to. And then aging happens. You don't notice right away, since you've been preoccupied becoming. The first physical signs appear in the mistress of the universe's head. That hair that was aflame with success is turning a smoky gray. The next change is attitude, if you're lucky. You still *can* but you no longer *want* to do it all. This is a good thing. It means that you can be a real mistress of the universe and put other people to work. But when you've always done everything yourself, it's hard to recognize that you don't have to when you don't feel like it.

Instead you beat up on yourself. You feel guilty about the dust buffaloes roaming the corners of the house and the yardwork you've let go from one season to the next. But there is nothing to feel guilty about. Let someone else do the work. Fuel the economy. For ten bucks someone will cut the grass. For a few dollars more someone will spring-clean the backyard and haul the trash away. What good was it becoming mistress of the universe if you can't delegate duties around your own castle.

SUBSCRIPTIONS

Subscribe to a home maintenance or home mechanics magazine. They talk about the things a homeowner needs and should want to know.

CHECKLISTS

Make them. Like junk drawers, checklists relieve the pressure of having to work everything out in your head. Merely checking off a finished item makes you feel like you are getting somewhere, and feel more in control. It creates a sense of well-being and accomplishment that propels you to the next step, even if as the list is shrinking from the top it is growing from the bottom. The psychology of writing tasks down and giving them a name makes big jobs approachable and more importantly, doable.

BE AWARE

It is important to develop a practical sense about safety at home. Install the triple locks on the doors, the chain-link guards on the windows, the monitored security system in every room, and a noisy dog with major jaws if you must. But you would be living pound-foolish and penny-wise if you don't also shell out the relatively few dollars it would cost to buy and maintain a fire extinguisher and smoke and carbon monoxide detectors. So many accidents occur at home, some fatal, because of a lack of awareness about the need for these simple safeguards.

So you have a **fire extinguisher.** Good. But how long have you had it? Does it work? What about the **smoke detector**? Is the battery strong? You should check the gauge on the fire extinguisher twice a year to see that it is reading in the green. Over time the fire-fighting agent, which is a dry chemical powder, can weaken. Also, the gauge may read in the green even if you've discharged it. Once you have used the extinguisher—even a little bit—it should be serviced or replaced because it loses its potency. If you put out a small fire with an extinguisher, it still may be a good idea to call the fire department. I know we don't want to draw attention to ourselves, what with all the commotion fire engines bring. But better the commotion than a tragedy. A mattress fire, for example, can smolder and flare up again hours after it appears to be out. You may have put out the fire on the stove but nearby electrical wires may have been affected and cause a fire in the wall the next time you attempt to use the particular outlet or switch. Better to be a safe spectacle than a sorry one.

A smoke detector is *worthless* without a charged battery. We've all heard the tragic fire stories about how the smoke detector was present in the home but it was without a battery. Check the smoke detector monthly for battery strength. Many of these devices have self-check features where the detector gives off an obnoxious high-pitched whine when the battery is wearing low. The only way to stop the noise is to remove the old battery and **INSTALL A FRESH ONE IMMEDIATELY.** Unfortunately, I feel obliged to yell that at you because there are university-educated folks who have a string of alphabets at the end of their name who remove the dying battery to stop the racket but either don't feel pressed to replace it right away or they simply forget. It can be a fatal omission. Be certain that the smoke detector is loaded with a working battery. Keep a spare handy in the refrigerator to maintain its freshness. Check the detector every six months, or else time the checkup to the change to and from daylight savings time.

Another household danger that escapes the attention of many is **carbon monoxide,** a colorless, odorless toxic gas. Because it can neither be seen nor smelled, I call it the stealth killer. About half of carbon monoxide poisoning incidents occur within homes. Carbon monoxide poisoning produces flulike symptoms in its victims, who often complain of fatigue, headaches, and runny nose. Extended exposure to the gas causes irritability, dizziness, disorientation, nausea, breathing difficulty, chest pain, convulsions, coma, and ultimately death.

Carbon monoxide is created by the incomplete combustion of wood or hydrocarbon products that are produced as a by-product of burning almost anything. In a house the source typically is a fireplace, a wood-burning stove, or a space heater operating in a room that is not well ventilated. When you use your gas stove to heat a room, you are risking carbon monoxide poisoning. Using a charcoal grill indoors is a risk. The only treatment for a victim is huge doses of fresh air. Seek emergency medical treatment as soon as the symptoms are present.

Develop a Seasonal Maintenance Schedule

I know it sounds like drudgery. That's because it is. But create a list that you can return to every few months and check off items, and it won't be so bad. Winter is ideal for inside jobs. You could, for example, recaulk the tub and shower and get rid of those gawd-awful mildew stains that built up on the grout that you promised to do every time you took a shower. A good mildew-removing solution is to mix one cup of household bleach with one quart of water. Sponge it on the tile wall and soak the grout seams where the bacteria builds up. Scrub the grout with a stiff bristled toothbrush. You may have to repeat the process a few times until it works. When the grout is clean and dry—in a few hours—apply grout sealer to the seams. Of course, if you washed the shower walls and surround with a detergent every third time you showered, you wouldn't have to undertake such a major production.

Every home has its own particular needs. However, there are a few maintenance standards that ought to reside on every seasonal checklist. Here is a sample to get you started. As you get to know your house, you will become familiar with what house functions need systematic preventive attention and repair.

FALL

- Install storm windows.
- Caulk around windows.
- Mow the lawn one last time to shred the last of the fallen leaves. The leaves can be left on the lawn if they are mulched into small enough pieces. This eliminates raking and bagging.

- Drain remaining gasoline from lawn mower into a gasoline container. Store the container somewhere outside of the house.
- Clean and repair sagging and or leaking gutters and downspouts.
- Check snow removal equipment—shovels, blower—to be certain they are functioning.
- Flush toilets periodically in seldom-used bathrooms to prevent gas buildup from sewer.
- Bleed hot water radiators.
- Inspect and or install insulation around doors and windows.
- Inspect attic for signs of leaks and other openings.
- Look for loose bricks and mortar on chimney. Have the chimney professionally swept and inspected.
- Clean window air conditioner filters and put protective cover on unit for season.

WINTER

- Replace smoke detector batteries.
- Check furnace filter.
- Inspect sight glass on furnace of steam or hot water system for rust buildup. To prevent rust buildup, flush the lines and drain the furnace in a steam or hot water system once a month or once a week if temperatures are severely cold over an extended period.
- Inspect radiators for malfunctioning steam valves. Replace if necessary.
- Check outside faucets for drips and assure they are completely off. Water trapped in an outside line can freeze and seriously damage pipes inside.
- Look for frayed appliance and lamp cords.

SPRING

- Check air conditioners and central air. Clean condenser, replace filters.
- Change or wash filter on range hood. Clean fan blades and housing.
- Clean refrigerator drain pan, vacuum condenser coils.
- Check hoses on clothes washer for firm placement in drain hole. Look for leaks.
- Vacuum lint from clothes dryer ducts.
- Check positioning of downspout to be sure it is properly seated in the dry well or directed onto a splash block or other rain diverter you may be using.
- Clean gutters and reseat loose lengths.
- Inspect lawn mower.
- Install door and window screens.

SUMMER

- Have fun!

There is always something to do around a house. Just knowing how things work and what the many parts of the house and its systems are called is the first major step in empowerment. No need to live a life as a Do-nothing Diva because someone made you believe that is your destiny. If you live in a house, it needs you. Learn what it needs, take care of it, and it will take care of you. It worked for me and it will work for you. Happy hammering!

Glossary

Baluster. A vertical spindle or spoke that supports a rail, such as a staircase handrail.

Balustrade. A row of balusters topped by a rail.

Boards. The name the construction world prefers to call slats of wood.

Bead. Expression for an application of caulking. Applying a thin application of caulking around a window or in a crack is to "draw a bead."

Bind. What you get into when you run out of choices. It also is what happens to a tool that is hindered from operating freely such as saw blades and drill bits that get stuck in the wood or plaster midspin.

Blind stop. A thin strip of wood placed vertically along the jamb of a window. Together with the parting strip and inside stop, the blind stop creates the channels that keep the upper and lower sashes of a double-hung window on track.

BTU (British Thermal Unit). The quantity of heat required to raise the temperature of one pound of water one degree Fahrenheit.

C-clamp. This clamp, shaped like the third letter of the alphabet, is used to press two objects together or hold an object firmly in place.

Chalking. A clever self-cleaning process developed in high-quality exterior paint that gradually turns the surface layer of paint chalky. Dirt that adheres to this chalky surface layer is periodically washed away by rain.

Cold chisel. A type of chisel made of a resilient strength, shape, and temper suitable for chipping or cutting hard metal or masonry.

Countersink. To drive the head of a screw or nail just beneath the surface.

249

Cure. The process of drying out or maturing material. Also the hardening or seasoning of cement or mortar.

Damper. A valve inside a duct or flue used to slow or stop the flow of air or smoke.

Dry well. An underground draining system for diverting groundwater away from a house's foundation. Sometimes the wells are made from perforated oil drums that are weighted down with concrete blocks or stones.

Eaves. The lower border of a roof that overhangs the wall.

Efflorescence. Water-soluble salts that are washed to the surface of masonry, forming a crystallization.

Fascia board. The board that covers the joint between the eaves and the top of a house wall.

Female. An object bearing internal threads, such as a nut that is designed so that another complementary object (male) can be inserted.

Flashing. Sheet metal or copper used in waterproofing the joints between a chimney and a roof and along the roof joints themselves.

Flue. A channel in a chimney designed to conduct flame and smoke to the outer air.

Foot. More than one foot is *feet* everywhere but in construction, where a footage measurement is expressed in the singular, i.e., "The plank is twenty-five-foot long."

Footing. The base on which a masonry wall rests to provide even distribution of the wall's weight.

Frost line. The depth at which the ground freezes beneath the surface.

Glazier's points. Tiny metal triangles used to hold a windowpane in place.

Hawk. A mason's hand tool used to hold mortar while repointing bricks.

Header. A beam that forms the upper support for a frame or wall.

Hip. The name of that part of the roof where two slopes meet to form a ridge.

Leveling. To make even or uniform.

Male. An object with external threading, such as a bolt, that is designed to be joined with another object with internal threading (female).

Member. Refers to one or more of the joining components of a construction. For example: The top and four legs are the members that make up a table.

Mortar. A mixture of cement, lime, sand, and water that hardens and is used in masonry or plastering.

Mud. The construction world's term for a plaster mixture.

Muntin. A strip of wood separating panes of glass in a window.

Parge. To apply plaster waterproofing to a wall.

Parting strip. Part of a three-member assembly that keeps a double-hung window on track.

Percolate. A method of testing the composition of the earth on a proposed building site for suitability for construction.

Pitch. Slope or angle of a construction.

Plumb. A measurement that is precisely vertical or true.

PNS (popped nail syndrome). When nails in walls and ceilings loosen and push through as a house settles.

Pointing. The process of chiseling out old mortar from between brick joints and replacing with new material.

Rabbet. A channel, groove, or recess cut into of an object, such as wood or metal.

Rafters. The parallel beams that support a roof.

Rip. Cut. It's more studly to say you are going to "rip some boards" than "cut some planks."

Running foot. A continuous line of measurement unbroken by angles and curves.

Saddle. Another name for threshold, which is located at the bottom of an exterior door.

Sash. The framework in which panes of glass are set in a window or door.

Setback. The distance a building must be constructed from property lines.

Sheathing. The first layer of boards or waterproof sheeting on the outside wall of a frame house or on a roof.

Shim. A slim piece of material, usually wood, used to make a loose fit snug.

Sill. The horizontal member at the base of a window; also the threshold of a door.

Skin. The building trade's expression for the exterior facade of a building.

Spline. A long, very thin strip of wood, metal, rubber, or plastic inserted in the narrow grooves of a screen to hold screening in place, much the way the spine of the human body works.

Square. When two objects are at right angles to each other; also the name of the tool used to determine if an area or object is square.

Stool. The correct name for what is popularly called the windowsill.

Stud. A vertical length of wood or metal (2x3, 2x4, or 2x6) spaced at sixteen- to twenty-inch intervals in a wall to which sheathing, paneling, and/or wallboard is fastened. (Also a man with high muscle definition.)

Strike plate. That part of a door lock assembly that is attached to the doorframe so that the tongue or latch of the lock fits into it when the door is closed.

Subfloor. The sheets of wood that provide the support beneath a finished floor.

Subroof. The framework that supports the foundation beneath the main roof.

Sweat'n da joint. Joining two metal pipes by heating and melting solder along the joint using the flame of a butane torch.

UL (Underwriters' Laboratories). An independent agency that performs safety tests on electrical appliances. Their sign of approval inspection labels are found on nearly every electrical appliance.

Valley. The name for that part of the roof where two slopes meet and form an elongated depression.

Water closet. Popularly known by the general term, bathroom. However, in the plumber's world, it is a quaint term of art of European origin referring specifically to the toilet.

Weep pipe. Think of the human tear ducts. This is a small pipe with a very narrow opening that gradually channels water buildup away from a foundation wall. Such a device would be used, for example, in an air-conditioning unit that is built into an outside wall to guide water runoff from the unit away from the building.

Resources

EPA Factsheet: Home Garden Beneficial Species. Environmental Protection Agency, 401 M Street NW, Washington, D.C. 20006.

University of the District of Columbia Cooperative Extension Service, 4200 Connecticut Ave. NW, Washington, D.C. 20008.

Maryland Cooperative Extension Program, Home and Garden Information Service. 1-800-342-2507.

Maryland Department of Natural Resources, 580 Taylor Avenue, Annapolis, MD 21401.

The Wilderness Society, 900 Seventeenth Street NW, Washington, D.C. 20006-2596.

U.S. Fish and Wildlife Service, Department of the Interior, 1800 C Street, Washington, D.C. 20040.

Brown County University of Wisconsin Extension Service—Storm Sewer Tipsheet.

Anne Arundel County Department of Utilities, "Save Water, Maintenance and Money . . . And Help Save the Bay" by Elizabeth Brabec.

Creative Homeowner Press, "Quick Guide to Plumbing" (1992), 24 Park Way, Upper Saddle River, NJ 07458.

Creative Homeowner Press, "Quick Guide to Wiring," 1992.

Creative Homeowner Press, "Quick Guide to Walls and Ceilings," 1992.

Time/Life, *Fix It Yourself: Lighting and Electricity* (1994), Sunset Publishing Corporation, Menlo Park, CA 94025.

Better Homes and Gardens, *Do It Yourself Home Repairs* (1985), Better Homes and Gardens Books, 111 Tenth Street, Des Moines, IA 50309.

Better Homes and Gardens, *Complete Guide to Home Repair, Maintenance & Improvement,* 1995.

Reader's Digest, *Complete Do It Yourself Manual* (1989), Reader's Digest, Dept. 250, Pleasantville, NY 10570.

The MacMillan Visual Dictionary (1992), MacMillan Publishing Company, 866 Third Avenue, New York, NY 10022.

Other Suggested Reading

"Composting: A Recipe for Success," Composting Productions, International. Marketing Exchange, PO Box 775, McHenry, IL 60051.

"Let it Rot," by Stu Campbell. Story Communications, PO Box 445, Schoolhouse Road, Pownal, VT 05261.

"Pesticides and You," National Coalition Against Misuse of Pesticides, 701 E Street SE, Suite 200, Washington, D.C. 20003.

Index

Page numbers in italic type indicate illustrations.

INDEX

INDEX

INDEX

INDEX

INDEX

INDEX

INDEX

INDEX

ALLEGRA BENNETT is a journalist and former television political commentator and editorial writer with the *Washington Times*. She created the *Renovating Woman* column, which has appeared in the *Washington Times*, the *Baltimore Sun*, and various other newspapers. Her home repair tips were featured regularly for two years on WBAL Radio in Baltimore, and she appears twice monthly with loads of repair, renovation, and maintenance advice on a popular morning variety show viewed on WMAR-TV in Baltimore. She has produced a 1997 calendar, "Renovating Woman, Fabulously Fifty Plus," celebrating women aged fifty and older. Also a budding stand-up comic, Allegra lives in Baltimore.